Shades of

VIOLET MAY
Record Collector's Corner

Broad Street, Sheffield
Tel. 54215

Remembering Sheffield's Vinyl Goddess

Violet May

by John Firminger & Gus M. Chapman

Published by youbooks.co.uk
11 Riverside Park, Sheaf Gardens, Sheffield S2 4BB
Telephone 0114 275 7222
www.youbooks.co.uk

Every effort has been made to check the information and find copyright for this book.

Foreword *

"Violet May was a pivotal figure in the development of the music scene in Sheffield. Not only in what people bought in terms of records for their listening pleasure but in how that music influenced countless musicians as well. Without her I'm sure that I wouldn't be making music today, although I never had the pleasure of meeting her but my father did and some of the music he bought in her shop still informs many of my ideas to this day. She widened the sonic palette of thousands of people from Sheffield and other places in Britain as you will see in the pages of this book. In this age of instant access to virtually any recordings at the touch of a button it is hard to imagine a time when you could spend months, often years, tracking down a rare record by an obscure artist you may have heard only snippets of their music, or had a cursory and rather vague knowledge of, but it really was like that and Violet May was a light in the darkness for the avid record collector and the developing musician. How she got those records is still a mystery to me and this book, written by my good friends "Gaspin" Gus Chapman and John Firminger, at last sheds some light on that closely guarded information. My Father found records by Howlin Wolf, Muddy Waters, Little Walter, The Dell Vikings and many, many more which at the time were virtually impossible to find over here, and the effect they had on a young enquiring mind was like a cerebral atom bomb. I still have those records my father left to me and I for one would like to thank Violet for them and the stories I keep with me always, along with her effect on the broadening of her customers musical horizons which is incalculable, although as a hard business woman I doubt she ever knew. I wish she and her spirit of adventure was still with us, the world is a duller place without people like her, and I truly hope you enjoy this book as much as I did, it's a labour of love - a thing as rare as some of Violets records - and almost as hard to find."

Richard Hawley

ACKNOWLEDGEMENTS

Sheffield Newspapers
Radio Sheffield
Windmill Records
J. P. Bean
Niko Reuvenkamp
Martin Bedford
J. Wrigley

Contents ✳

COLOUR PLATES:
Violet at 30 years old - 33; 78 rpm gems from Violet's - 34-35; Record retailers sleeves - 36; Rare extended players - 37; Violet's holiday snaps - 38; More rare 78's from Violet's 39; Violet's record shop locations - 40 - 46; Old map of Park District - 47; Sheffielders on record - 48; Celebrities who visited Violet's shop - 52; Hero worship - 54; Cool jazz album display - 56; Trad Dad at Violet's - 57; Blues at Violet May's - 60; Sheet Music at Violet May's - 61; Violet's name revived - 84-85.

Introduction ✳

Sheffield has always enjoyed the presence of various characters and personalities, especially during the last 50 years. People connected with music, the arts, sport, industry or just adding a bit of colour to the city's general ambience have made their mark in varying degrees and their efforts will be remembered by many for their contributions.

One such person was Violet May, the lady who ran a series of new and second-hand record shops. She is indeed well remembered by many serious music fans whose frequent visits to Violet's shop would generally bring rewards of obtaining a rare gem or indeed some further enlightenment. Situated in several different locations, Violet's shops were very much part of the music scene in the 60's and early 70's and created her own niche amongst musicians and music fans. Recalled especially by the more discerning fan and collector as she would cater for their various tastes, managing to obtain the more obscure items in the process. Whether it be a rare jazz album, an obscure classical 78 or some small independent label, Violet would invariably come up with the goods. She is also remembered with mixed feelings for the way she ran her shops and treated customers. With an almost dual personality, Violet could switch from being a most cordial proprietor to being a most rude and hostile person towards any customer she simply didn't like the look of. However some of this hostility has ironically made her more remembered by all those who'd experienced these mood-swings. As shown in the brief look at her personal life, she continued to be quite domineering and at times pretty exasperating right up to her death. But in her defence, as our story shows, her demeanour was as a result of her traumatic and complex early life.

In order to preserve some of these memories, we take a look back at the years when Violet operated her shops and include the recollections of other past customers and collectors as well as members of her own family. Talking to the various people it's obvious that Violet May certainly left them with some quite profound recollections, as well as some highly prized records. They were also very enthusiastic and encouraging towards the idea of putting this book together and our sincere thanks to everybody who has contributed. Just like it often was in one of her shops, we hope you enjoy the visit back there, but please leave your carrier bag behind the counter!

John & Gus.

Some of the photos used in this book are of varying quality, having been taken from old video tapes, but we feel are still most significant.

Enter Violet May

Violet May Timms was born 26th August, 1910 in Daniel Hill Street, Upperthorpe, Sheffield, and was one of three children. The daughter of Frank and Emily May, the name Timms in fact had Jewish Greek origins and as a child she led a hard life due to her tyrannical father as Violet's daughter **Grace Monk** recalls; "Her father was awful to her, and her brother Charles and sister Ivy." In view of this all the family left home at the earliest opportunity. "Ivy married the first lad she had for the same reason. Ivy left home at 17 to get married and went on to have two boys. Frank joined the air force to get away," In fact Frank Timms is noted as being the youngest navigator in the RAF during the 2nd World War. Whilst their father was a tyrant, his wife, May, is remembered as being a docile and lovely lady. In retrospect Violet inherited some of both her parents attributes as daughter **Joyce MacDonald** reflects; "If she had only married someone who was really loving, she would've been a really good partner for that person." By her teens Violet had grown up into an attractive, yet free-spirited young woman and in 1926 demonstrated this by leaving home and moving to London. Here she worked at a hotel and also as a store-detective. Also, according to Violet, at one time during in these 'salad' days she had done some photographic modelling for the 'Green Goddess'. Not the Army Fire Engine but a brand of ladies' cocktail drinks. **David Timmins**; "It was a bit like Creme De Menthe in looks but a totally different taste. It was made in Rotherham and was popular from the 30's and was still around in the early 60's. It was one of those drinks that was an acquired taste and was tried out once; I think there was more left in the glass than drunk. Green Goddess was favoured mainly by women and if they did acquire the taste then they drank it regularly. I didn't know Violet May had modeled for the drink but it doesn't surprise me."

The actual picture used to advertise the drink shows a naked young girl covered only by a see-through chiffon and on reflection would certainly have raised a few eyebrows if this is how Violet looked in her photographs as well as questioning her claim! Helping to substantiate this is a photo of a twenty-something Violet looking quite demure although only a head and shoulders shot, but the expression on Violet's face is certainly that of a glib young nymphet!

Left; The original Green Goddess advert whilst Violet's pose (right) is a little less revealing, the photo is signed 'With all my love Vi'

After moving to Hull around 1929, Violet started seeing a young student and after she became pregnant she wanted him to marry her but as daughter Joyce recalls; "She was in Hull and she was engaged, or certainly had a big romance with a student Doctor and his parents said 'if you marry her then we won't see you through University.' He was doing his degree in one of the Scottish Universities, either Edinburgh or Aberdeen, training to be a Doctor, and he then had nothing more to do with her."

In 1930 her first daughter Joyce was born and for a young single woman with a baby back then, things would certainly have been hard for Violet. Added to this, her baby would apparently scream constantly, day and night, creating further problems for Violet and as a result she found it difficult to keep her job. Her only solution at this time would be to have her baby daughter fostered out. **Joyce**; "Violet was 20 when she had me. I was adopted when I was only 10 months old as in those days it was impossible to keep a child. Grandad (Violet's father) wouldn't help her when she had me, he wouldn't even see me until I was eighteen and he never accepted me.

I was fostered by some people in a place called Summerscale Street in Hull for a while. Violet visited a few times until I went to Doctor Barnardo's Home at some point. After announcing 'Baby Girl for adoption to a good home', at the Home, I was legally adopted by James Henry Pearson and his dear wife Mabel.

They had three sons but always wanted a daughter and so the arrangement was very amicable." **Joyce**; "They just jumped at the chance and they went along and by ten months, it was official and Violet had to be in the court to hand me over, physically, that's what they did. Naturally she was upset and said, 'can I keep in touch with you?' And being my Mum and Dad, they were the salt of the earth, the loveliest people. They were in their 40's when they adopted me which was quite late, but they did want a girl. I was so lucky to have them."

Violet then met Peter Elsworth from Leeds. He couldn't marry her as he was already married, but separated from his wife, and in those days he couldn't get a divorce if his wife wouldn't agree. So the two lived together in Scunthorpe and in 1932 had a daughter, Grace. Four years later the couple had another baby, this time a son, Peter. Joyce recalls; "We lived in a place called Mona House in Hull and we sometimes came to stay with Violet and Peter, I used to call him Uncle Peter, that's Grace and Peter's father, in Scunthorpe.

When I was about six or seven, I used to come to Scunthorpe for holidays. Mum and Dad brought me on the bus and left me for a week and I played with my cousins, Grace and Peter, I remember we were very happy." I thought they were my cousins, I didn't know they were close family." However, Joyce, Grace and Peter were to become much closer; "We'd only been a couple of times during the war until one night she (Violet) was in a queue with Peter at the old Savoy (Cinema) in Scunthorpe. And they'd heard somebody saying that they'd heard on the radio that a family in Hull had been wiped out and it had said that this elderly man and woman and little girl had been killed. They had a friend called Mr. Copley who had a car. I was about 11. We were at home in Hull and this car turned up and of course she (Violet) was in tears because she thought I'd been killed and the wipe out of the beginning of her life. Anyhow she couldn't let us stay there and she wanted to bring me to Scunthorpe and my Mum wouldn't let her and she said 'well you come as well Mabel' She said 'I don't want Joyce in all these bombings, we'd been bombed out three times. We'd been evacuated three times, we'd had it rough,'" Joyce continues; "It finished up with Violet and Peter, Grace and little Peter and my Mum and me all living in a three-bedroom house in Cliffe Closes Road, a very nice place in Scunthorpe."

In 1943 Violet quite surprisingly joined the ATS and moved to London on her own, taking her son Peter with her. **Grace**; "I never knew what she did with him. My father looked after me himself. Then Mr & Mrs Pearson who had adopted Joyce came to live with us as evacuees, so I got to know my sister." Joyce was of course oblivious to the fact that Violet was her Biological Mother until one day when she was setting the table for tea. "Graces' and my job was to come home from school and set the table. I must have done something different and Violet just said 'what are you setting the table like that for?' I said, 'that's how my Mum told me to do it'. And she said, 'your Mum? I'M YOUR MUM, SHE'S NOT'!!!! That's how I found out. I couldn't believe it, I went to pieces." Such a discovery was naturally a devastating one for Joyce. "I was just never the same again because I'd inherited, if you like, three big brothers who all spoilt me rotten and my Mum and my Dad and suddenly I wasn't part of them. That was the worst moment of my life." How did Joyce now feel towards Violet? "I can see her point because she would have seen me saying 'oh Mum, so-an-so' and she's watching this and I'm waiting for my Mum coming home from work.

Doing her bit - Violet in her ATS uniform

Violet (second from right) with daughter Grace, Mr Ainsworth and son Peter

I'm sure that afterwards she would have regretted it because she said, are you going to call me Mum now? I said 'no' and she said well you know I am your Mum' I said 'yes, you said so, but I'm not'. And she said 'well I can't make you but you and I know.' And I said 'yes, you've said so'. How did Joyce's maternal Mother react? "She didn't over react. She was of the old-school, she'd had three sons missing in the war for so many weeks and do you know she never made anything of it and she'd just say 'they're busy in the war'."

Down in London, as the war raged on, many parts of London were under attack. Where Violet now lived the entire street was bombed with only her house remaining, although, as son Peter recalls, "she was blown from the front door to the back door in the blast". Living in such a vulnerable position Violet decided to move herself and her son back to the relative safety of Sheffield in 1945. Upon returning she set about finding somewhere to live as Peter recalls; "We came back to Sheffield, to Walkley Street and lived in one room, that was terrible."

After settling back she would start up her own business by opening her first shop on South Road selling second-hand clothes. In 1946 she moved the business down to the busy shopping area of Burgoyne Road where she continued dealing in second hand goods again and some records. **Grace Monk;** "I did not see a lot of my mother from being about 8 up to the age of 17, so Pete was the only one close to her in those years." With whatever little success Violet made of the business, she was able to move to a larger home in Crofton Avenue, Hillsborough, in 1948.

After seven years apart from Violet, it was much easier to get a divorce when Peter Elsworth met a Mrs Scott. They moved down to Weston-Super-Mare with daughter Grace; "I met my husband in 1948 and we were married in 1953 after he had done his two years National Service in the army." Grace lost contact with her father after he and his wife went to live in Bournemouth.

In 1950 Violet began a new venture by starting up a toy factory outside of Sheffield at Penistone. Here she concentrated on making wooden rocking horses but unfortunately this venture failed as a result of the emergence of plastic coming onto the market. **Peter Elsworth**: "She couldn't compete, they cost that much to make. They had a spring at the front and she had to have springs specially made at Sheffield Spring Company." 1950 saw Violet and Peter move to the Drive, Marlcliffe Road, Hilsborough. The following year saw another move to Barber Wood House where Violet lived and worked as the house-keeper. Another move is reported, this time to West Street where Violet worked, again, as house-keeper to a dentist.

On reflection it would appear that Violet was a most restless person throughout her entire life as she always seemed to be on the move, on two fronts, whether it was to a different shop or to a new home she was constantly flitting from one place to another.

Junk to Records - the Early Shops

Still lingering from the depression days of the 30's and the 2nd World War, the Park District of Sheffield was notorious for its poverty and poor housing and, as told in J.P. Bean's celebrated book on Sheffield Gang Wars, in the twenties it had been a place where various unsavoury characters were based. It was perhaps due to the area's financial climate that this was where Violet would resume her own business buying and selling second-hand clothes, etc.

Returning to her role as shop-keeper in 1954 Violet opened a junk shop on South Street at the old premises of one-time barber Charlie Parkin. Charlie was well known in the Park district for cutting kids hair where it was said that he stuck a basin on an urchins head, went round with the hairdressing tackle and charged a threepenny dodger [thre'p'ny bit / three old pence] for the privilege.

As Gus recalls this was Vi's first shop in the Park District and it was located just above Granville Street on the right hand side of South Street as one walked up. There was derelict property below it and open space above it where other buildings had once been between her shop and the railway cutting - almost opposite what later became The Pavement shopping precinct. It was at these premises that Gus first encountered the lady. Along with a pal called John Steel, Gus made his first ever purchase from Violet's shop when they both bought an old cutthroat razor apiece and as they walked up South Street slicing a spud Gus inadvertently sliced a lump off his thumb! Shortly after he had recovered enough they nipped back and got a refund, albeit somewhat reduced it should be noted. Violet's next move would be not too far away on Duke Street where she had a shop on the right hand side looking up and was set back from the other buildings in the midst of a row of about six old terraced houses. Due for demolition it was sited between Maypole's and Gallon's grocers' shops, Gallon's being on the corner of Norwich Street. This was a dingy, pokey little place and she sold all sorts of old clothes and junk, some of which were on display outside. I was always a bit wary in that shop because it never quite seemed safe to me amidst the adjoining derelict properties. The other shop on Duke Street was above the Bernard Street / Talbot Street Junction, just a little way above Hampton Street, [now known as Manor Oaks Road], and was on the opposite side of the street to the other one. Just above was the pie and pea shop where all the starving kids used to go after they'd been for a swim at Park Baths - and then the pie & peas would be swimming - in Henderson's!

Dave Theaker also remembers the neighbourhood with great affection; "Actually I was born in the Park in 1946 on Talbot Street, where I lived until I was 10 and a few minutes walk from Violet's old shop on South Street. I was mildly gob-smacked to hear that I'm not the only person in this world who can remember the pie shop. My Mum used to send me there with a basin. Behind the pie shop was Sky Edge which was like a mini Wild West/Arizona. I spent hours up there playing round the open cast mine and pig farm. We lived next door to the Black Horse pub and next to that was Mrs. Dawson's sweet shop. There was a Doctor's surgery on a nearby corner just below the baths. The doctor who I saw was Doctor Hart."

For a short while Violet had a shop on City Road, which is actually the same road but changes name at Robinson Road - a little way above Vi's old shop. This was just below Granville Road, again on the right hand side looking up and was an end terrace. I'm not sure whereabouts this fitted into the shop progression and it's a place I rarely visited but it probably slotted in between the two Duke Street shops.

Whilst her turn-over from the shop was limited, in order to supplement her income Violet took a job as a store detective in the city centre department store of Cole Brothers. It was here that Gus had his second encounter with Violet. I was around 15/16 years old which would be sometime around 1954. I had gone in and was having a merry old time lifting various items of model railway equipment and stuffing my pockets with them. When I thought I'd satiated my fetish enough I made my way out of the main door and started down the street when a voice called to me asking me to return to the shop as she thought I'd taken some items without paying for them. I naturally protested but it was to no avail as she was accompanied by a male assistant. It was of course Violet - and she was the store detective! I ended up going to court and had to pay a fine which didn't please my old man too much. Obviously I didn't know her at this time and she couldn't have made any connection in later years because nothing was ever said and I didn't realise that it was her who had made the collar that day until she dropped it out in the shop once that she'd been a store dick in the said store up town. You could have knocked me down with a Hornby Dublo!

Alan Spinks recalls the rare occasion of getting one over on Violet, albeit dishonestly; "I was born in the old Park district and I remember well her shop on Duke Street just below the Park baths. In the late 50's all my friends had a bike except me so I felt left out; as my dad couldn't afford to buy me one. One summer's evening in 1958 I was walking on Talbot Street towards the old Norfolk cinema when I spotted a bike left outside the old Black Horse pub, I jumped on it and pedaled off to the old houses where the Park hill flats are now and hid it in one of the empty houses. I now had a bike so I could go cycling with my pals. Eventually my dad bought me a bike so I now had to get rid of the stolen one.

So off I went to Violet May's and told her a cock and bull story about my dad being skint and wanting to sell his bike for £1.00. She offered 15 shillings but I told her my dad said to take nothing less than £1 so she told me to go and get a signed letter from my Dad and she would give me a £1. So I wrote a letter myself and when I took it back to Violets she said 'I don't believe for one minute your dad wrote that letter you probably wrote it yourself and for that I'm only giving you 15 shillings.' I snatched her hand off - I fully expected her to accuse me of stealing the damn thing. I gave my 2 pals half a crown each and off we went to the fair at farm grounds I was rich, I'd never had so much money in all my life, we had a great time at the fair. A few weeks later two school pals, Harry Richardson & Graham Ashton got caught shoplifting up town and they snitched on me and I got fined £1 at the juvenile court and my poor old Dad had to pay the fine."

For Violet the second Duke Street location was somewhat more substantial and it seems it was here that she started to get more into the records side of the business, although she still traded in junk. In an article in the Star Violet recalls how she began selling records; "I used to buy things at salerooms and sell them in the shop, then one day somebody brought me a pile of old 78rpm records. There must have been about 200 and I kept them in a little wooden box my husband made for me. They sold so quickly that I decided to advertise for more. People kept bringing me collections and it just grew from there."

Duke Street in 1964; Violet's shop became W. Burgin & Son with the plain fronted one above being the welcomed hot pie shop

It would be from some of these collections that John recalls such items as the Gene Vincent & The Bluecaps album displayed in her window in order to attract a wider clientele. **Dave Hawley;** "It became apparent that you could buy anything from a cheese sandwich to a pocket-battleship, records were a sideline." **Alan Wood** recalls one particular attraction in Violet's window; "After I'd been to the swimming baths and got my hot pie from the pie shop, I used to gaze at this colour photo of Tommy Steele. I saved up my pocket money and went and bought the photo and took it home to which my Mother said, 'you've spent your money on that?' she didn't understand."

Dave Hawley; "From the mid 50's to the 60's, the availability of American records was almost nil. Many were released but only the most commercial succeeded. The others were never plugged and finished up in junk shops all over England." Back in those early days Violet admitted that she knew very little about records; "I gained knowledge as I went along. I learned a lot from my customers."

Chris Spedding; "Both Rich Smith and I used to buy our jazz records from her. We went there every time we had some spare cash. And she gave a good price on part exchange! Not much more I can remember but we spent many an enjoyable Saturday morning browsing in her shop. She would always play us records we wanted to hear before buying. Very nice lady, This would be around 1959/60."

Chris Spedding

Rare American Releases On The London Label

(1) Classic R&R Doo-Wop, (2) Phoenix Rockabilly
(3) From the legendary Sun label

Dave Berry; "Violet's shop provided myself and many other local musicians with the records that we learnt many of the songs from that we'd go on to perform onstage. These would often be the more obscure ones by names like Muddy Waters and Roscoe Gordon that weren't readily available in any of the other record shops."

The shop on Duke Street was the place where Gus first really got to know Violet as he only lived down the street apiece and he started doing odd jobs for her now and then - and this would signal the start of a long, and often at times stormy, friendship. At around this time Violet married William Barkworth and the two lived in a house on Martin Street, which took Violet back to Upperthorpe and the area she was born in. Bill was in fact the cousin of the well known film and television actor Peter Barkworth. He also had the distinction of being the first man Violet had actually married. It's also a coincidence that three men who were associated with Violet all had worth in their name - Elsworth, Ainsworth and Barkworth, indeed for Violet it must have all been 'worth' it.

(Below left) Violet's cousin by marriage, stage and screen actor Peter Barkworth
(Right) Bill Barkworth, Violet's son Peter Elsworth and Violet.

Record Rendezvous *- The Pavement

Beginning in 1957, most of the Park area was being transformed from its grimy mass of narrow back streets of densely populated two and three storey dwellings, passages and courtyards into a modern and revolutionary housing complex. The centre-piece of this new development would be the Park Hill Flats, a futuristic looking block of 995 flats rising up to 4 storeys high at the top end to 13 storeys at the bottom end nearest the city centre. This resulted in the largest housing complex of its kind in Europe and was a virtual 'Streets in the Sky'. The new Flats had been officially opened in 1961 by politician Sir Hugh Gaitskill and also included amongst this development was a shopping area called The Pavement. It would be here where Violet's next move would be to just down the road from her previous shop.

In comparison this was indeed a more up-market location, and also in keeping with the times. Virtually brand new, Violet's shop was situated upstairs on a gallery with a name that would fit in with its modern surroundings and was called the 'Record Rendezvous'. The shop's interior was quite up to date too, befitting of this revolutionary (as some called it) new concept in living.

Peter Elsworth; "I did all the work, tiled the floor and put some booths in for listening." Here Violet's business had now become a full-time record shop and in fact had the modern look and displays of the other Sheffield record shops like Wilson Peck's, Philip Cann's and W. H. Curtis. Unfortunately, despite its modern image, Violet's husband Bill was left in charge but is unfortunately remembered by some visitors to the shop as 'being on another planet most of the time'.

The Pavement, Violet's shop was at the far end of the building just left of centre in the picture - up on the balcony

Peter Elsworth; "He was running that Pavement shop but he hadn't got the push for it, didn't have the know-how and as a result the shop suffered." Maybe this was another reflection of Violet's blind-side when it came to business or simply keeping her costs down. Unfortunately as a result of this and probably the high over-head costs, the Record Rendezvous only operated little more than a year before Violet was on the move again. More conducive to the younger generation however and adding to the Pavement area's new musical ambience was the Zodiac Coffee Bar. Here teenagers would congregate to while away the hours making a cup of coffee last as long as they could while keeping the juke-box on continuous play.

TOP TWENTY

WEEK ENDING FEBRUARY 14

	Title	Star	Record Company
1	Jailhouse Rock	Elvis Presley	
	Story Of My Life	Michael Holliday	RCA
3	All The Way	Frank Sinatra	Columbia
4	Oh Boy	The Crickets	Capitol
	At The Hop	Danny and the Juniors	Vogue-Coral
	Great Balls Of Fire	Jerry Lee Lewis	HMV
7	Peggy Sue	Buddy Holly	London
8	You Are My Destiny	Paul Anka	Vogue-Coral
9	Ma	Johnny Otis/Marie Adams	Columbia
10	My Special Angel	Malcolm Vaughan	Capitol
11	April Love	Pat Boone	HMV
	Bony Moronie	Larry Williams	London
	Love Me Forever	Marion Ryan	London Nixa
14	Kisses Sweeter Than Wine	Jimmy Rodgers	
15	Kisses Sweeter Than Wine	Frankie Vaughan	Columbia
	Bye Bye Baby	Johnny Otis	Phillips
17	Reet Petite	Jackie Wilson	Capitol
18	I Love You Baby	Paul Anka	London
19	Magic Moments	Perry Como	Columbia
	Story Of My Life	Gary Miller	RCA Nixa

COMING UP FAST ... I'm Left, You're Right, by Elvis Presley HMV

Compiled from dealers' returns from all over the country

TOP TWENTY

Compiled from dealers' returns from all over Britain
Week ending May 28, 1960

No change for top two... but Brenda Lee and Cochran are challenging

Last Week	This Week	Title	Artist	Label
1	1	Cathy's Clown	Everly Bros	Warner Bros
2	2	Cradle Of Love	Johnny Preston	Mercury
5	3	Sweet Nuthin's	Brenda Lee	Brunswick
9	4	Three Steps To Heaven	Eddie Cochran	London
6	5	Handy Man	Jimmy Jones	MGM
4	6	Do You Mind?	Anthony Newley	Decca
7	7	Shazam	Duane Eddy	London
3	8	Someone Else's Baby	Adam Faith	Parlophone
	9	Footsteps	Steve Lawrence	HMV
14	10	Mama/Robot Man	Connie Francis	MGM
15	11	Sixteen Reasons	Connie Stevens	Warner Bros
11	12	Heart Of A Teen-age Girl	Craig Douglas	Top Rank
10	13	Fall In Love With You	Cliff Richard	Columbia
16	14	Stairway To Heaven	Neil Sedaka	RCA
12	15	Stuck On You	Elvis Presley	RCA
18	16	I Wanna Go Home	Lonnie Donegan	Pye
	17	The Urge	Freddy Cannon	Top Rank
13	18	Standing On The Corner	King Brothers	Parlophone
	19	That's You	Nat 'King' Cole	Capitol
	20	Let The Little Girl Dance	Billy Bland	London

ONES TO WATCH

You'll Never Know What You're Missing — Emile Ford and The Checkmates
Lucky Five — Russ Conway

Mike Cocker; "I first heard of Violet May's shop in 1964 when I was aged 14 from somebody (can't remember who) at my school (King Edward's). I think I first went there shortly after with others on the way home from school."

*Dust and Shellac - back to South Street

After about eighteen months, at the most, Violet vacated her shop on The Pavement and reverted back to older premises again and, signalling a return to South Street, was situated directly below the old Park Cinema. After the modern setting of The Pavement, this was a much lowlier place, now called Record Collector's Corner, and was in fact a bit of a shit-hole. Quite a step backwards for Vi, it was quite organised as a shop, albeit crammed with LP's, EP's and 45's. The room upstairs was filled with 78's but this fact wasn't helped either by the lady herself who let the place simply become an unorganised mess.

Glyn Senior "What blew my mind was the upstairs which was full of 78's. Boxes and boxes of the buggers. I spent ages looking through them but cannot to this day remember one title. They were obscure to say the least. Nobody ever came upstairs to check up on me and to my knowledge nobody ever bought a 78." In the centre of the room was a record player on which customers could listen to a particular record they'd found. The only trouble was, everything was in such chaos it was hard trying to locate a specific artiste as the records were simply all either shoved onto shelves or stacked in piles. However, this sometimes had its benefits as while you were looking for one artist's records you might come across somebody else you were interested in and keep shooting off at various musical tangents!" Although this was part of the appeal in going to Violet's it was like digging for buried treasure as you waded through hundreds of dusty old records, often leaving the place with very dirty hands.

Phil Robinson; "My old man got a 78 from her, 'Gandpa's Spells' by Jelly Roll Morton, with a hand-written label, it was an aluminium disc with shellac laid on top, God only knows where she got that stuff!"

South Street, Violet's shop was the premises directly below the Park Cinema

Mike Kersey; "I think I went in all of her shops at some time, as a schoolboy I used to cycle to her shops whenever I had a few bob to spend. I was just buying the hits of the day like Elvis/Cliff/Adam Faith and Lonnie Donnegan etc. She was selling singles at 3 shillings about half price what they were uptown so I could buy twice as many. A bit later when I started work at 15 and had a bit more money I started trying to get a complete collection of Elvis records and I had started collecting EP's as I loved the sleeves, also The Beatles and Stones and the beat groups were taking off so I was also buying these."

Criminologist and author of the celebrated Sheffield Gang Wars, **J.P. Bean** also recalls finding a rare gem amongst those shellac oldies, "I remember being very excited at finding a Hank Williams 78 in the upstairs room, "Leave Me Alone With The Blues"/"Tears In My Eyes". It cost me four bob (four shillings - 20p) and I thought I'd struck gold. This was in 1965, I was into old Hank in a big way but nobody else seemed to be at the time - certainly nobody my age - I was 15. I thought it was a great discovery." Unfortunately J.P.'s excitement was short-lived. "I left it on a chair and my Mother tripped up over my guitar case and landed in the chair and broke it into about 10 pieces! She wasn't bothered in the least about my record. I said, 'Mother, it was priceless and it's broke!' But all she would say was how she could have hurt herself. I tell you, I'd got more tears in my eyes than Hank Williams sang about."

Dave Theaker: "Amongst the records I bought early on were "Smoke Gets In Your Eyes" - The Platters, "Feel So Good" - Big Bill Broonzy. A lot of 45's by Ray Charles; "What'd I Say", Phil Upchurch "You Can't Sit Down". My pal Billy Carr bought loads of stuff and knew Violet May better than I did.

Hank Taylor: "Not knowing as much as I do now, I often wonder what gems I left behind, because the artists' name was not familiar to me."

Hank Taylor with a copy of 'Leroy' by Jack Scott, one of the 78's he picked up at Vi's

As well as records, Violet continued to sell other goods and **Phil Brodie** recalls buying his first guitar from her South Street shop. "I looked at it in the window and at £10.00 it was a lot of money at the time as I was only ten years old. It was a white Rosetti Lucky 7 and I'd been watching it for a week and the sun had split the corner of the body as the guitars were made of plywood. and somebody had glued it together. I pointed this out to Violet and managed to get it for £9.10s.0d. (£9.50) but Violet was a very sharp business woman and did the deal very sharply."

Dave Hawley; "By 1960 the Sheffield scene was shaping up and it was becoming obvious which bands would remain commercial and which musicians would become Sheffield's rockers, blues and country musicians. The latter started to meet every Saturday lunchtime in the Stone House pub on Church Street opposite the Cathedral and just up from Coles Corner.

The talk would be about the favourite styles of music and the different venues that the musicians were playing that night. Over a period of time the conversation would shift towards this shop that had suddenly fallen out of the sky - Violet May's"

AND THE FAMOUS LUCKY 7!

In red, white or turquoise; fine leather strap in the price: Superb tone, Only **12½ Gns.** (plus 3/7 extra purchase tax).

LIFE IS SWEETER WITH A Dansette

You'll love the tone of these smartly styled Dansettes— deep rich reproduction that makes your records sound twice as good.

DANSETTE POPULAR
Fitted with the latest BSR 4-speed mains motor and turnover cartridge, the Dansette Popular plays all your records, whatever size or speed. And the amplifier is fitted with independent tone and volume controls. 11½ Gns. (Inc. P.T.)

DANSETTE CONQUEST AUTO
A truly luxurious set. The high quality two-stage amplifier and two 7" matching speakers give you magnificent reproduction. You have independent bass, treble and volume controls, and the latest in 4-speed auto-changers. Open or closed, it plays up to ten of your records— any size, any speed. And you can use it as a portable, table or standing model. 24 Gns. Inc. P.T. (Legs optional: 2 Gns. extra.)

Both models offer you a variety of two-tone colours to choose from—and a full guarantee by Dansette. See them at all good radio shops and leading stores.

Collectors Corner* - Broad Street

Another move around 1965 saw Violet go a short distance from South Street down the road and round the corner to set up shop in equally old premises at 30 Broad Street. Situated between Lizzy Benson's Lino & Carpet shop on the corner of South Street and the Plough public house, it was perhaps in a more prominent place than its predecessor had been.

The old Sheffield Corn Exchange, Violet's shop was just hidden round to the right of the building.

For Sheffield this was quite a historic spot as it was near here, where the River Sheaf met the River Don, that Sheffield began as a small agricultural settlement around 800AD.

On the opposite side of Broad Street was the old Corn Exchange and a pub called the Exchange, but known locally, yet mystifyingly, as the Maunche. Inside the shop, there were two rooms, front and back with a toilet right at the back. The back room was used mainly as a tea mashing area. Both rooms were jam packed with records, the counter area was a sea of vinyl 45's sorted into label order rather that artist. Upstairs were more records - mainly old 78's, but these were still pretty much in vogue at that time. Any LP and EP albums were separated from the covers and stored with a number written on the inner sleeve which had a corresponding number written inside the album cover. This was obviously to prevent light fingered merchants from making off with illicit goodies, but the system was not completely foolproof as on odd occasions the numbers didn't match up.

Violet May's Collectors Corner. Shoppers looking into Violet's Broad Street Shop window

Violet's husband Bill would continue to help out in the shop. He would hardly ever say anything to anybody apart from a few mumbles between him and Vi but he was an okay sort of bloke who spent most of his time at work.

Peter Elsworth; "Their private life comprised of Mother watching telly." Unlike many of us back in the 60's, Violet also would enjoy the luxury of travelling everywhere by taxi, whilst back in those days, most of us would only fork out the extra cost of a taxi as a means to get home after the buses had finished. However, Violet always travelled this way to and from work and also for going out to concerts.

Another member of Violet's staff was Vera Ingram, the small lady who would clean the shop and generally be Violets runaround. Unfortunately she often came in for a verbal lashing if something she had done did not meet with Violet's approval. She was often humiliated by Violet, often in front of customers.

On his regular visits to Sheffield in the 60's, London collector Hank Taylor also paid numerous visits to Violet shops. "Funnily enough, my Mother's maiden name was also Violet May. My first trip to Violet's shop was during 1968 whilst on a visit to Sheffield to meet up with Gus and John. The shop she had at the time was situated at Broad Street and upstairs was a treasure trove of 78's, all neatly racked out and waiting to be purchased. I visited the shop many times during the late 60's with Gus and spent a lot of time digging through those 78's, purchasing items by Merle Travis and Tennessee Ernie Ford on Capitol, Bill Haley on London, Pee Wee King on HMV and Jimmie Rodgers on Regal Zonophone. I must admit that there is nothing like the smell of a room full of 78's, it is a smell you only get with shellac!"

As well as the different musical categories that the records were in, there was also a box full of odd singles. Located just inside the door, most of these records were without sleeves and were of varying condition. We would always check out what was in the box and did come across some items that have since become quite collectable. So as not to block the doorway, and of course when she was in a good mood, Violet would sometimes tell us to take these odd singles and go through them upstairs. Gus recalls one overcoat inside pocket that just happened to be 45rpm size that would prove useful for slipping certain selected records into and afterwards just return the rest back in the box, telling Violet that there was nothing worth buying! Next door to Violet's shop in Broad Street was The Plough pub where we would often go for a pint to wash down all the record dust and to check out our booty! **Howard Holmes;** "When I was fifteen me and a mate discovered Ray Charles at Violet May's record shop in South Street, and Violet then turned us on to Chuck Berry, Bo Diddley and the Chess R&B artists. We said thank you by nicking 45's from her shop. Sorry Vi." **Muriel Elsworth;** "I used to be serving and I'd see people put things down their trousers. And she'd say 'keep an eye on him.' They used to go up stairs for hours and hours and she'd say, 'you better go up and ask him if wants a cup of tea while he's up there'" **Glyn Senior;** "Everybody from the R&R scene went there. That's where the guys bought the records to learn the songs. The best time to go was on a Saturday afternoon, after the pubs had shut."

Kenny Roper; "On Fridays, I remember the Pye Rep would call and bring in the new Pye records by Chuck Berry and Bo Diddley."

Amongst the many Sheffield musicians who would gravitate to Violet's shop were Scott William, Dave Hawley, Ron Blythe, Dave Berry, Chuck Fowler, Joe Cocker, John Riley, Dave Hopper and disc-jockey Gaspin' Gus who ran the weekly rock'n'country sessions under the heading of The Sun Sound Club at various venues in the city.

Some of Violet's Rockin' customers

THE STAR TOP STARS SPECIAL, October Edition.   3

TOP STARS POLL 1964

NATIONAL

Top Male Singer

1. ELVIS PRESLEY   2. Dave Berry
3. Cliff Richard   4. Chuck Berry

Top Girl Singer

1. CILLA BLACK   2. Brenda Lee
3. Dusty Springfield   4. Kathy Kirby

Top Group

1. THE BEATLES   2. Rolling Stones
3. The Searchers   4. The Kinks
5. Manfred Mann   6. The Hollies

LOCAL

Top Male Singer

1. DAVE BERRY   2. Jimmy Crawford
3. Joe Cocker   4. Johnny Tempest

Top Girl Singer

1. KAREN YOUNG   2. Pat Leslie
3. Gaye Saxon   4. Ray Carpenter

Top Group

1. THE STAGGERLEES   2. Joe Cocker's Big Blues
3. Sheffields   4. Knives and Forks
5. The Cruisers   6. The Lizards

TOP DISC JOCKEY

1. JIMMY SAVILE   2. Alan Freeman
3. David Jacobs   4. The Stringfellows

BEST DISC

1. "THE CRYING GAME" Dave Berry (Decca)
2. "You Really Got Me" The Kinks (Pye)
3. "A Hard Day's Night" The Beatles (Columbia)

(left) Chuck Fowler, Frank White,

(Right) Scott William and Dave Berry

(Below) A smiling Violet surrounded by potential buyers

Joe Cocker (left) recalled one humorous memory of Violet's shop when he listened to a new Howlin' Wolf album she'd got in. After playing the album Violet commented, "She's very good, Howlin' isn't she?" Unknowingly she'd obviously thought the young black chick on the cover of the album was actually the person singing on the record! Many of Violet's regular customers were quite diversified in their tastes but she was usually very conversant with her clientele's various tastes in music.

Mike Cocker; "It was clear she had a great interest in pre-Beatles pop and a full knowledge of the stock she carried."

Dave Theaker; "Violet can't be appreciated enough on the music scene in Sheffield in general. For those who liked Chess, Atlantic, Blue Note, R&R, Bluegrass and Blues, the main problems were actually getting to hear the music and then finding somewhere to buy it. Violet was the most authoritative and knowledgeable shop owner. Canns on Chapel Walk was OK but at the mercy of staff that had no knowledge of US R&B. Barry at Wilson Peck's was helpful but he didn't have the buying flexibility that Violet May had. Violet often amazed me; she was just an ordinary looking little old lady but she knew her stuff and her shop was the ONLY place in Sheffield where you could find new Blue Note - Lee Morgan, Jimmy Smith, Art Blakey; Chess - Muddy Waters, Howlin' Wolf, Little Walter, etc. She was always ready to spin you a track if you asked her nicely."

Gus also recalls two elderly gents who frequented the shop and were classical music fans. At first they used to look down their noses at us. However, Violet was pretty good at getting material on record that kept them coming back for more and after a while we eventually got on nodding terms with the two 'classical cats' as we had dubbed them.

Violet and Gus

Violet's shop was also popular with the jazz fraternity as she was something of a jazz buff herself with Louis Armstrong being a particular favourite and would attend many of the jazz concerts at the City Hall. However, **Ron Blythe** recalls another of her musical preferences, "She really loved The Platters and that sound." "I like any good music", she commented in 1978, "I'm particularly partial to jazz, but I like listening to anything that is good in its field."

Our musical penchant? well we were rock'n'country enthusiasts, listening to the likes of Carl Perkins, George Jones, Jerry Lee Lewis, Buck Owens, Little Richard with then, a more snobbish attitude towards most other forms of music. However, here again, regardless of her own musical preferences, Violet kept her ear to the ground regarding any new releases of our kind of music.

It was at the Broad Street shop where Violet started to make a name for herself as an out-post for good music outside of Sheffield. As quoted in the Sheffield Star, her name was becoming known with the bi-line; 'from Sheffield to Tin Pan Alley'.

This was reflected on one memorable Saturday afternoon around the Summer of 1967 when the then up and coming band Fleetwood Mac made a special personal appearance in Violet's shop. Why they didn't choose one of the bigger shops up town like Cann's or Wilson Peck's is a bit of a mystery, or maybe it was due to Violet becoming an outlet for the newly formed Blue Horizon

Fleetwood Mac

label for whom Fleetwood Mac recorded. Their initial single was "I Believe My Time Ain't Long"/ "Rambling Pony" (Blue Horizon) and began to achieve some success with "Black Magic Woman" and "Need Your Love So Bad". Naturally their appearance attracted lots of people who mingled with the band getting autographs and possibly buying copies of their record, whilst John and Gus recalled "we looked on, thinking 'who are these guys?' Little did we know, or anybody else for that matter, just what an important and successful band they would become, especially in their much later re-incarnation.

Best-Selling Blue-Beat L.P.

"I FEEL THE SPIRIT"

Prince Buster (BBLP802)

Send for free catalogue of Authentic Blue-Beat records

BLUE-BEAT RECORDS

12 Earlham Street

Another area of music that Violet became one of the first to cater for in Sheffield was Ska or Bluebeat. This music was initially aimed at many of the young Jamaicans who lived up nearby Pitsmoor and Burngreave who this music appealed to before it became more generally popular. These recordings would feature names like Prince Buster, Don Drummond, Desmond Dekker, Freddie Notes & The Rudies. **Dave Theaker;** "She certainly had a reggae period when the shop was full of young Jamaicans buying the latest releases from Kingston. I didn't go in on the weekends much during that period as I couldn't stand the bloody row, but if I did go in Violet would just roll her eyes at the reggae and direct me to the blues section." **Muriel Elsworth;** "When that come out, 'Big Five', reggae, I was always playing it cos' I thought it was funny. And she (Violet) would say 'stop playing that'!" **Peter Elsworth;** "There used to be half a dozen records come out every week and she used to get em' all and they took over. They were there at the front where she sat, there were hundreds of em'."

Soul music also began to get popular and in order to keep up with this Violet began stocking many of the Atlantic - Stax releases, therefore attracting many of those who were into this music. **Dave Manvell**, "She got me a copy of a Willie Mitchell on Stax. Pete Stringfellow had a copy which he played at the Mojo and I thought the only way to get a copy was through Violet May. It was an import and the band were unknown." On one occasion she played one Atlantic single for a young fan and it turned out to feature country singer/songwriter Wayne Kemp which he instantly turned his nose up at. However we thought it was marvellous and made an instant purchase!

Introducing a new 'POP' label

'KING'

Releases on the new 'KING' label will consist of the pick of recordings by leading AMERICAN and CONTINENTAL stars.

FIRST RELEASE — AVAILABLE NOW IN YOUR LOCAL RECORD SHOP

DOWN BY THE RIVERSIDE
COME ON LETS SLOP
By EDDIE and the CRAZY JETS KG 1000

TWO NEW RELEASES IN THE 'BLUE BEAT' IDIOM

HOLD ON by Harris Seaton
.PEACE & LOVE by Lester Stirling   JB 143

RHYTHM OF THE BLUES
SIMPLE THINGS by Lord Creator   PJ 4005

KING RECORDS DIVISION OF
R & B DISCS LTD.

282b Stamford Hill, London, N.16   STA 4127

RHYTHM & BLUES GOODIES!

DADDY ROLLIN' STONE
DEREK MARTIN   SUE WI - 308

MOCKINGBIRD
INEZ FOXX   SUE WI - 301

SO FAR AWAY
HANK JACOBS   SUE WI - 313

I CAN'T STAND IT
THE SOUL SISTERS   SUE WI - 312

LAST MINUTE PART ONE
JIMMY McGRIFF   SUE WI - 310

SEND FOR ME
BARBARA GEORGE   SUE WI - 316

and . . .

INEZ FOXX IS COMING. . . .

More satisfied customers; Gus and Scott William check out some new rockin' sounds on record

Lol Widdowson: "The Sheffield Star newspaper was running a competition called 'Pick The Spot' in which they printed some pictures of shops from various locations in the city." The prize was a 45rpm single from Violet's shop and Lol, along with his brother Ian, won it twice, from which point Violet barred them from entering the competition anymore. One of the prizes they won was a Chris Montez single - groovy eh?

Lol was working at Timpson's shoe shop on Pinstone Street and on pay day he would go down to Vi's and blow all his hard earned cash on records. "On arriving home and explaining the situation I would get a top notch rollicking from my mother. Another recollection was the time that there was a downpour and both Gus and I were trapped in the Broad Street shop because it was flooded outside and we couldn't get out the darned place for quite some time. Violet kept us amused by playing some of our favourite records."

Hear Me Talkin' — Violet May

Here follows a transcript of an interview with Violet which was published in The Sheffield University Jazz Club Magazine, February 1967:

Violet May Barkworth runs the only shop in Sheffield that caters for the Jazz record specialist. A visit to her Emporium is a pre-requisite for anyone interested in the Recording Scene. She talks here to Maureen Williams (and Andrew Shone).

Maureen Williams - how long have you been in the record business?

Violet May - I had a general Shop since 1946, selling all kinds of goods, then a request for original 78's of any kind just 12 years ago gave me the idea of buying a collection of classical 78's, which I sold so quickly I decided to buy whole collections, whether classical, jazz, blues, or pops, by advertising and recommendation.

M W - Your stock has certainly expanded.

V M - Yes, I believe I have the finest stock of 78's in the country. Originals are in great demand - there's something about an old disc of any kind which seems to have mellowed with time - just try Bing the 'Old Groaner', Caruso, even Bill Haley on those original Rock 'n' Roll 78's. From all these you get today's pops, Blues and Soul', searching for an expression of our inner selves through the turmoil of wars, strikes and any evil which exists, and always will, human nature being what it is.

Andrew Shone - You see your shop as a bastion against evil?

V M - Well, 'Say it with Music' gives us all our own satisfaction, and feeds 'the Soul'. How many of us in any generation hear a tune almost forgotten in the archives (and which you will probably find in my shop), a tune which reminds you of a loved one, a nostalgic moment of courting days, in fact "memories are made of these".

A S - very true

M W - Why don't you run a mail-order service?

V M - I wish I had the time. I could make a fortune. I get requests from Singapore, Her Majesty's Prisons, the Blind - a lot of my customers are from out of town, London especially. They come on personal recommendation, as I've advertised only in 'Vintage Jazz Mart.' High Brows, Low Brows, all browse at Violet May's Record Collectors' Corner - the only one of its kind in Sheffield, and why? Behind it all is just an insight into human nature, and the Public getting the impression that, if Violet May hadn't what you wanted, then she'd "get it".

M W - You've not always been at Broad Street have you?

V M - No, I came here fairly recently. Before that I was round the corner in South Street, but it was my Duke Street shop that made my name. I liked it best - I was there for five years. My present place is four times as big as South Street, but still not enough. Demolition keeps me on the move, and I'm afraid I'll be forced to move again fairly soon. Of course, lack of space stops me from putting everything in their proper categories, though I *have* separated the cheaper Jazz labels.

M W - What part does the Jazz side of the business play?

V M - The Jazz clientele is one part of the public, though inexplicable lack of support makes the local Scene poor, compared with other cities of similar size.

A S - Oh?

V M - Yes, in the post-war era there was a reasonably large following, but it petered out in the early 60's. Jazz is not catered for in Sheffield, apart from the odd Jazz concert at the University, thereby letting the 'Outside' In. It's a great pity about Jazz in Sheffield. We are missing the 'Greats' of our time in the flesh, unless we're prepared to travel to Birmingham, Leicester or Manchester.

M W -Do you get many customers from the University?

V M - Wednesdays and Saturdays the shop is full of flying scarves. I'd say 80% go for Folk, 20% for Jazz. 95% of sales are LP's, though they do buy lots of New Orleans Jazz 78's. Part exchange is very important in the jazz turnover.

A S - Significant.

V M - I have the special imports; labels like Pirate, Transatlantic, Blue Note, Heritage, Electra, Xtra are scarce in Sheffield. Most of the 78's I get are from private collections. I bought all the 78's from the old Empire when it closed down. The jazz 78 section upstairs is very large, and well worth looking through.

M W - What sections of Jazz sell well at present?

V M - Well, of Trad, the 20's period is very popular, also Errol Garner and the M.J.Q. Sales are 50/50 Trad and Modern, some of my Modern customers are very selective. John Coltrane is very good.

A S - What about the Avant-garde?

V M - Only about 10% of total jazz sales. I don't like the way out music at all - it doesn't signify anything, it's not getting anywhere. People are listening for something that's not there. I'd say there's a definite trend to Big Bands - Harry James, Benny Goodman, Artie Shaw, Lionel Hampton, Basie and Ellington. I like all swing myself. Jimmy Smith is very popular. 50% of my Blue Note sales are by him

A S - Really?

M W - What of your own personal collection?

V M - "I'm very selective, though I have a bit of everything. I particularly like Tchaikovsky, Chopin, operas like 'Tosca' and 'La Boheme'.

M W - Have you any special hobbies?

V M - I love painting. I started when I was 18. Sometimes, when I'm in the mood, I get up in the middle of the night. Crazy!

M W - Tell me something of your family.

V M - I'm the eldest of three, with a brother and sister. I've three children and six grandchildren.

M W - Do many famous names come to your shop?

V M - Acker Bilk, Dave Berry, Davy Graham, John R.I. Davies, Sadlers Wells, Black and White Minstrels, Ray Nance, George Lewis, Bud Freeman, Edmond. Hall, Cecil Payne, Wild Bill Davison, Johnny Griffin, and many more. Why? - they're all in the search for music of the soul, and they'd have a better opportunity, my stock is so varied: Big Bands, Avant Garde, Classical, Soul Ballads, Rhythm and Blues, Imported Discs, even a 6d. record for the Old age Pensioner, Six months ago, I even had a gross of old phonograph cylinders; they all went within a fortnight, all old artists, unknown today. What is life without music? I myself have no preference, whether Jazz, Classics, Blues, or Pops - if the artist has 'soul' it must be good. When I need relaxation, according to my mood I play any record with this in mind.

M W - Jazz as well?

V M - Jazz records pay for themselves if you are selective and just buy the ones which convoy the message to you - this then *must* be good music.

A S - How so?

V M - The soul message was in the discs of 50 years ago, and it's so apparent even now. Our teenagers love this music, and consider they are "with it" when they little know they've never been without it. I don't care for present 'pop' really but it needs someone to stock what the public wants and needs. One of my customers in London wanted a military march 78. I played the record over the 'phone, he liked it and that was that. Incidentally, I've never known George Formby records to sell like they have been over the past couple of months.

M W - Who would you say has been your most impressive customer?

V M - Believe it or not, Ray Ellington. A smashing personality, easy to talk to. I remember Jimmy Rushing as well. My customers are my friends. I like to give personal service, and feel genuinely interested in their desire to get away from it all in the 'Sound of Music'.

M W - I see you have a collection of reference books and catalogues.

A S - Are they for reference?

V M - Yes, including Brian Rixs' "Jazz Records, 1899 - 1931", a really useful book, and I sell secondhand jazz magazines as well. The 'Record Mirror' once asked me to compile a list of R & B and Folk. I used to stock new jazz magazines, but nine months left a lot of them on my hands. The University one always sells out, though - I'm very impressed with it.

"Swing-cerely",

Violet May

This interview has been reproduced with kind permission of The Sheffield University Jazz Club Magazine.

JAZZ

CLUB
MAGAZINE

SHEFFIELD
UNIVERSITY

NUMBER 3
FEBRUARY 1967

Violet on the Web

The following pages are extracts of fond memories posted on the forum website **SheffieldForum.co.uk**

Chris M

I spent most Saturday mornings in the late 60's early 70's trawling round all the second hand record shops and market stalls around town. One of my haunts was Violet's store at the back of the Moor (I did visit her old shop a few times down near what is now Castle Square) What a place - never mind the records the banter between the punters and Violet was priceless. She was a wily old bird - although she often miscalculated the value of some of the Soul imports/demos she had in the shop - so I picked up some bargains. Who was the old guy who worked there - he was on other planet most of the time. She once had a float in the Lord Mayors Parade and sat in a rocking chair at the back of the truck. I presume Violet is no longer with us.
Happy Days.

Bushbaby

I managed to get "Breaking Down The Walls of Heartache" by Edwin Starr on Import, from Violet's. It was for the Youth Club's Northern Soul Disco.
I liked it in there as browsing was welcomed. Lots of Jazz freaks in striped jerseys talking about Brubeck and the Newport Jazz Festival.
It was where I first heard of Billie Holliday, who I'm now a big fan of.

goldenfleece

I recall the shop well, used to search for back catalogue old 45's when I was a DJ.....Violet ALWAYS had copies of everything that had ever been in the charts in the 50's and 60's. The shop was piled to the roof with brown wooden boxes crammed with 45's, with the name of the label on the front of the box.
She used to puff away at her fags in real chain smoking style, the whole shop was a fog of smoke at the best of times......but what an atmosphere and great customer service. Saturday mornings at the shop were an essential part of life for any DJ in the 70's who wanted to complete their oldies record cases.
She was a bit bad at adding up though and I always got everything dirt cheap.

tiffy

I remember as a kid when my sister wanted a particular record as she had joined the school choir and needed to rehearse at home. So for a few weeks we trudged down the moor to Violet May's shop and although we never got the record we enjoyed browsing without any hassle from staff. Great days.

Madgeca

I was a 'Saturday girl' at Violet Mays back in the early 60's my mom's neighbour Alan Simmonite got me the job (which I got sacked from. I was a lazy little bitch back then), happy days.

PopT

Memories came flooding back when I read the letters with comments about Violet May. As a young teenager I used to go to her record shops in the early days searching for jazz records. One shop was on South Street opposite the Old Corn Exchange opposite the bottom of the old Rag and Tag market. She moved to a shop on City Road above Bernard Street. Later she moved to a corner shop at the back of the Moor near the Golden Dragon Chinese restaurant. She used a cigarette holder to smoke her cigarettes and seemed to have quite a collection of them, every I saw her she had a different one. She attended all the jazz concerts at the City Hall and cut quite a figure dressed in long dresses and smoking from a very long cigarette holder. She knew most of the musicians and her knowledge of jazz music was extensive. I remember her guiding my choice of records knowing what little money I could afford and I thank her for developing my education in the music. I once picked up two metal master cut recordings of Charlie Parker from her shop on City Road only to sell them back the following Saturday. At that young age I was disillusioned with them as they contained lots of false starts and stops. Little did I know that this was normal for 'The Bird', any jazz fan today would give his high teeth for those two unique recordings today. Does anyone else remember this Sheffield character and the early jazz days in Sheffield?

mojoworking

I was a regular at Violet's in the mid to late 60's when the shop was opposite the Rag market. I picked up loads of gems there, but the one I recall most strongly was a 10" LP by Jesse Fuller. I don't suppose many people have heard of him. He was a one-man-band blues singer. Donovan had name dropped him in a magazine interview, so I decided to check him out. Paul McCartney later recorded one of his songs (San Francisco Bay Blues) on his Unplugged album.

Speaking of Macca... I happened to be in Violet's shop in 1968 during the week that Hey Jude came out. It was playing continually on the little record player she had in the corner (the release of a new Beatles' single was a major event back then) and I couldn't help eavesdropping on Violet's conversation with another customer while I was browsing the racks. They were talking about Hey Jude (among other things) and Violet opined very loudly that it was "their best record yet".

As usual, she was spot on. Good old Violet.

Violet at age 30 years old

78rpm Gems from Violets

1.

2.

3.

4.

5.

6.

(1) Chuck Berry song performed by British folk/blues/skiffle pioneer of the 50's
(2) Great American blues shouter and pianist (3) Original recording of a pop classic
(4) America's Music Sweethearts; Les & Mary
(5) Rare solo disc by Hank Williams' band (6) Classic Elvis on HMV

7.

Brunswick
BROADWAY WOOD LIMITED
03618-A
IT'S BEEN A LONG LONG TIME
(Jule Styne, Sammy Cahn)
BING CROSBY with
Les Paul & his Trio
Vocal, with Instr.
Accomp.

8.

"HIS MASTER'S VOICE"
SPEED 78
B.D.1218
MY VERY GOOD FRIEND THE MILKMAN
(Burke—Spina)
"FATS" WALLER AND HIS RHYTHM
(Vocal Refrain and Piano by "Fats" Waller)
N.C.B.

9.

ZONOPHONE
THE FOGGY MOUNTAIN TOP
CARTER FAMILY
SPEED 78
5493

10.

PARLOPHONE
R. 4432
SPASMS
(Sinaw—I—Glover)
LITTLE WILLIE JOHN
and Chorus
CAMPBELL CONNELLY

11.

Brunswick
03744-B
YOUR SOCKS DON'T MATCH
(Carr, Crosby)
BING CROSBY with
LOUIS JORDAN AND
HIS ORCHESTRA

12.

Capitol
CAP6826
CL 13465
JOHN AND MARSHA
(Freberg, Stone, Liebert)
STAN FREBERG
Vocal, with Orchestral Accompaniment
CAMPBELL CONNELLY & Co.

(7) Bing sings with accompaniment from Les Paul (8) Classic from the great singer/songwriter
(9) Country music's first family (10) Classic piece of 50's R&B from the young pioneer
(11) A rare coupling of Bing and the great jump-jive king
(12) Wonderful slice of 1950's humour from the master of parody

One of Violet's old bags together with some other local record retailers of the past

Rare Extended Players

Rare British EP's picked up at Violet May's shops in the 60's

Released on the much loved London American label the Roy Orbison **HILLBILLY ROCK EP (1957)** *featured four of his early Sun recordings and now valued at £170. Rockabilly singer Ben Hewitt's* **BREAK IT UP EP (1960)** *featured two of his Mercury singles and now valued at £150. The two EP's by hillbilly singer Howard Vokes* **AND HIS COUNTRY BOYS (1962)** *and* **MOUNTAIN GUITAR (1963)** *were issued on the very rare Independent Starlite label and now valued at around £30/40 each. Another London release, Rick Nelson's* **YOUNG WORLD (1962)** *contained rare album tracks and now valued at £75. Issued on the short-lived Top Rank label, the* **COUNTRY MUSIC EP (1962)** *by country singer Frankie Miller featured four tracks from the US Starday label and now worth around £60.* **THE FABULOUS CHARLIE GRACIE (1957)** *Parlophone EP featured four hits by the great rock'n'roller and now worth £60. Vol. 6 of Top Rank's series of* **COUNTRY & WESTERN EXPRESS (1960)** *featured tracks by James O' Gwynn and Tony Douglas from the US 'D' label and now valued at around £50.*

Violet's Holiday Snaps

One of Violet's famous "paintings" (see article page 78)

More Rare 78's from Violet's

1.

2.

3.

4.
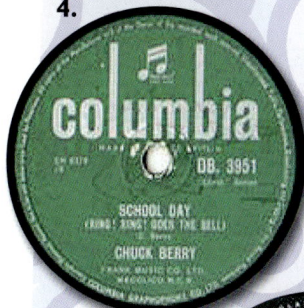

5.
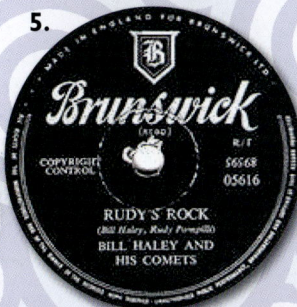

6.

7.

8.

(1) Hillbilly boogie from the ol' 'Pea-Picker'
(2) Instrumental boogie from the guitar great (3) the original doo-wop group
(4) Classic from the 'Rock'n'Roll Poet'. (5) Instrumental blast from Bill's band
(6) Country classic from the 'Hillbilly Shakespeare'
(7) Rare slice of 50's Nashville rockabilly
(8) Rare US 78 from the 'King of Western Swing.'

South Street

Violet's first shop in the Park district was a small property located here just below the footpath to Granville Street in between a space next to the wall and Charlie Parkin's barber-shop with no evidence left when area was redeveloped in the 60's

City Road

Just below the top of Granville Road; Violet's shop was the last one in the row of terraced shops (where the van is parked). The premises have now been transformed into private housing.

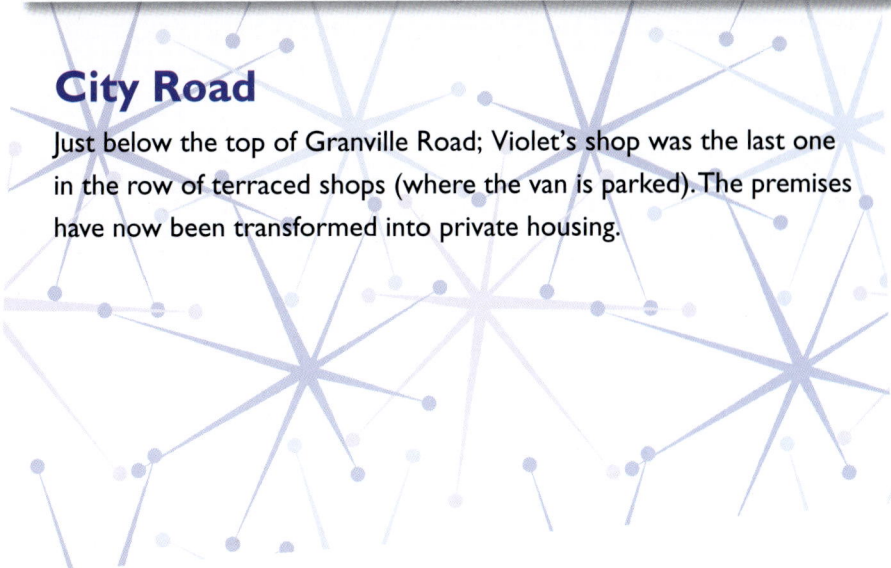

Duke Street

Situated just down the road from the Park Swimming baths and Library. Violet's shop was the top half of the continental fast food shop *Spicy Chef & Curries* with the old pie shop next door.

Duke Street & The Pavement

Violet's first shop on Duke Street was located just above where the Pavement was. In 2008 the Park Hill Flats underwent part renovation with the entire Pavement area having been demolished, and unfortunately leaving no trace of Violet's *Record Rendezvous*.

South Street

Looking down towards the lower end of South Street where Violet's shop stood just below the Park Cinema where the Supertram track can be seen, completely demolished and redeveloped as part of Park Square.

Broad Street

Violet's shop was under the fly-over just past where the small electric sub-station building is in the centre of the picture in the middle of Park Square roundabout.

Matilda Street

Built in 1969, Violet's last shop is thankfully still very much as it was when she had it (apart from the security roller shutters). Now catering for another set of collectors, the shop *Forbidden Planet* deals in fantasy and sci-fi memorabilia.

Photos: Gus and John

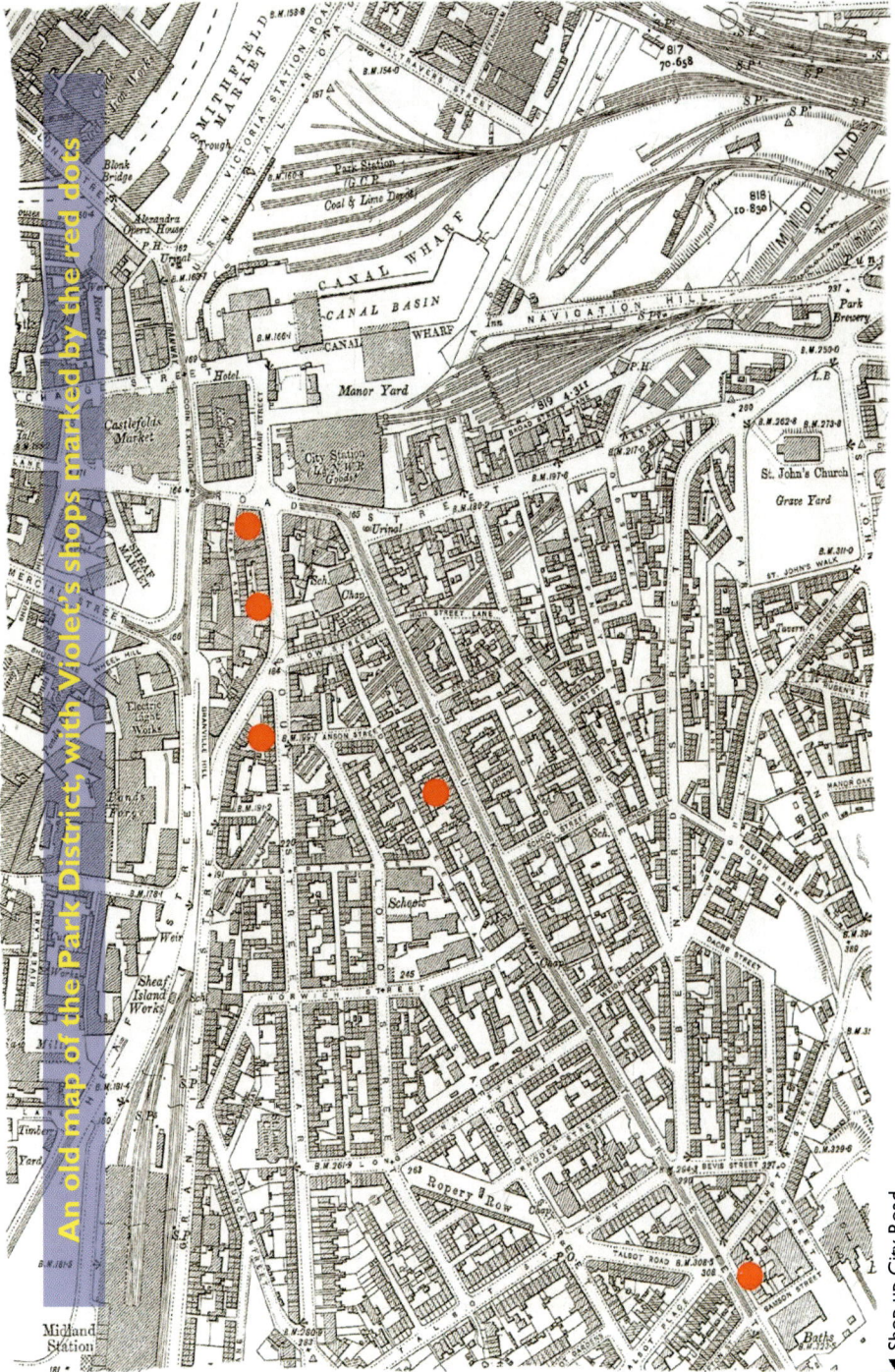

An old map of the Park District, with Violet's shops marked by the red dots

▼ Shop up City Road

Sheffielders on Record

Frank White was the only British artist signed up to Creedence Clearwater Revival's Fantasy label with his Nice To Be On Your Show album. The Texans featured popular local singer Johnny Tempest on a song written by Chris Stainton and Malc Towndrow. Husband and wife duo John and Ann Ryder cover a Simon & Garfunkel song. Dronfield's Karen Young's sad country chart hit. Sheffield's first chart star Jimmy Crawford with his cover of US hit. Crawford's backing band The Ravens Rock Group and a solo instrumental single of their own. Dave Berry's band The Cruisers and a single of their own with a cover of a Bob Dylan song. Sheffield Rag Record recorded live at Pete Stringfellow's Mojo Club and featuring four local bands. Joe Cocker's first record with a cover of a Lennon & McCartney song. Made In Sheffield featured local songwriters Frank Miles, Tom Rattigan and Chris Stainton. Dave Berry seen on the cover of his aptly titled 1968 album.

✳ Uptown - to Matilda Street

By 1968, work on the new Park Square roundabout was looming and whilst it would feature walkways and gardens, it didn't include Violet's shop, even though she may have thought it should!

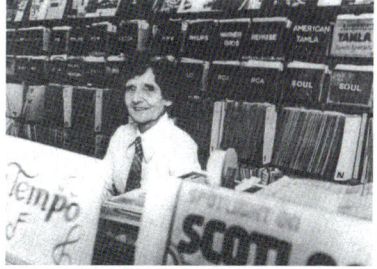

Therefore she needed to find another one and put her name down for a brand new shop that was still in the process of being built. Moving further up town and just off the Moor Violet's next location was on the corners of Matilda Street and Matilda Way. The new building was situated in something of an oriental setting with the Golden Dragon Chinese restaurant on one side and a Chinese fish and chip shop on the other.

Queen of all she surveys; Violet behind the counter in the Matilda Street shop

Gus's first view of this shop was from quite a different perspective. It was 1968 and the premises were just a shell with the upstairs joists running across - no stairs or anything else. I had gone in with my mate Pete Simpson to install the electrics - lighting, sockets and whatever, and we had to work from ladders. So I knew this shop literally inside out. We did this job at weekends and evenings as we both worked during the day and I can remember it being particularly cold and we usually had a visit from a friendly copper on the beat every night. The shop opened in 1969 and once again it was another well chosen location in a busy area and Violet soon established herself there.

Checkin' out some of the new additions in the Matilda Street shop

Checkin' out some of the new additions in the Matilda Street shop

One of Gus's first jobs in the new shop was (once again) to sort the thousands of 78's that her son Peter had carted from Broad Street and lugged upstairs. This was quite a mammoth task - bearing in mind that I had little or no idea who lots of the artists named on the labels were - but somehow we muddled through in an attempt to create order from chaos and confusion. Peter said that there was somewhere in the region of 10,000 of the things - and they were filthy to handle. Some of the labels that come to mind were the dark blue and gold Decca - dark red and gold Regal Zonophone - Capitol - Columbia - plum PYE - RCA - the ubiquitous London American label [black and gold and later black and silver] and many other varied coloured oddities which included some odd American imports with names like Bluebird and Starday and Capitol. Artists that spring to mind are people like The Carter Family and Jimmie Rodgers, material that we didn't amply appreciate at the time but were quickly scooped up by collectors and are probably worth their weight in gold now. Others included people such as Mario Lanza - David Whitfield - Doris Day - Frankie Laine - Caruso - Johnnie Ray - Winifred Atwell - Lonnie Donnegan - Tommy Steele - Elvis Presley with the odd pre-RCA light blue HMV label - plus many, many more in an endless list to be sorted into some sort of order. The main problem in regard to having and keeping them in order was the fact that the people searching through them quite often put them back in the wrong section, or just left them stacked in a pile on one side, thereby throwing them out of sequence again. There would often be small stacks scattered around the record player waiting to be reinserted back into stock. I spent quite a few weeks doing this, but I also performed various other duties for Vi - one in particular being any electrical problems she might have at her home on Cherry Tree Lane at Nether Edge. I'd catch a bus up armed with a few tools and when I'd done I'd usually call into the local pub before busing back to the shop. She used to have three or four lodgers staying at this house at that time and in view of this she'd had a telephone and coin-box installed - just a tin with a slot in it.

As well as being a member of Violet's auspicious staff, rock'n'country DJ Gaspin' Gus also hosted his own show on Radio Sheffield. "I actually used to plug Violet's shop on Radio Sheffield using the excuse that we got most of the records played from her shop whilst in reality a lot of them were actually American imports we'd picked up in London and some hadn't even been released here at that time."

The ground-floor of the Matilda Street premises appeared to be more organised as behind the counter were a lot of small drawers that would each have the names of the different record labels on and other categories.

Brian Monk; "It wasn't posh like record shops today, but had a great atmosphere and filled with people."

J. P. Bean; "I only went into the Broad Street shop once or twice, but later on I often went into Matilda Street. She seemed to have a very wide knowledge of records, from opera to folk and blues - all sorts. I can remember wondering if she'd listened to all the records in the shop and if so, how long had it taken! Bit of an odd thought really." **Peter Elsworth;** "One of the amazing things was, you could say the name of a record and label, and she knew the number, which is just fantastic." **Mike Kersey;** "I was also into Football in the 60's and she always used to have a good collection of back issues of Football Monthly magazines in the side window on Matilda Street so I used to buy quite a lot of these."

Violet's working day would begin at 9.30am when she opened the shop and carry on until closing time at 6.00pm. In that time she was behind the counter all day with little or no time to take a break. She told The Star, "I did try having lunch but it didn't work, I could not afford time to sit and eat." **Joyce Macdonald;** "She never ate much; she didn't eat enough to feed a bird. She said 'you'll have to forgive me not eating too much as I've got such a headache.' She said 'it's the ringing of those tills, it never stops'!" She always seemed loathe to leave the till area and it seemed as though she didn't have time to go to the toilet either! We always wondered if she wore a caffiter but having later found out that she didn't, she must have had a very strong bladder! The only times I recollect her going to the toilet was when she went to get changed for an evening out. **Joyce** "she never trusted anybody in the shop except herself."

Around 1970 Violet took part in a competition organised by CBS Records. It was for the best window display with a Country and Western theme and would be used to promote the label's latest C&W releases. Helping her to create a 'western-style' scene in her shop window Gus and John made up an imitation fire with a few sticks, red tissue paper over an orange light bulb and added a bit of sand.

Way out west; Violet's entry in the CBS C&W Records' Display competition

Celebrities who visited Violet's shop

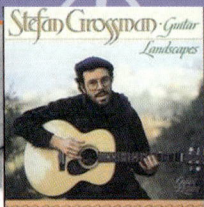

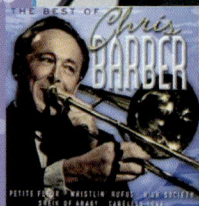

Folk troubadour Stefan Grossman, Trad Jazz'n Blues maestro Chris Barber,
Irish songstress and ambassador Dana, Blues great Jimmy Rushing
and Apple Records' Badfinger.

Carl Perkins & Gaspin' Gus

Margaret Palmer & Waylon Jennings

*Hero Worship

Some of Violet's customers meet their heroes in the 60's

ALAN MACLEAN & BUCK OWENS

BILL MONROE, CHUCK FOWLER & DAVE HAWLEY

WILLIE NELSON & JOHN FIRMINGER

Looking 'lonesome', JF models for Violets' display in her window

At the side was what looked like a guitar but was in fact a guitar-shaped electric wall-lamp! Against his better judgement, after being asked by Violet, John volunteered to take part in the project and acted as a model to give her display a bit more atmosphere. Posing amidst all the props and posters John sat provocatively trying to look 'lonesome' with a round piece of corrugated card-board with a hole cut out of it on his head in order to look like the brim of a cowboy-hat! Needless to say he felt anything but a cowboy, in fact - a complete knob-head! The things you do when you're young!

Hank Taylor; "One abiding memory of that shop was the day John Firminger was doing some window dressing to promote Vi's stock of country albums.

He cut out a cardboard circle, then cut out a hole for his head, then bending it in and pushing it back on his head to look like a Stetson! He clambered into the window space and sat down, I often think about that and it always brings a smile to my face." Fellow fan and collector **Pete Carson** took some photos of the 'display' for Violet to send in to the competition. Strangely enough, it appeared that our efforts were not a total waste of time and Violet's entry in the competition in fact came third. With this in mind, looking back, maybe John should have pursued a modelling career further!?

Glyn Senior recalls another event at Violet's shop, "One thing that always puzzled me was why the hell Apple Records chose Violet's for an autograph session when they were promoting Grapefruit (or was it Badfinger?). I saw it advertised in the Star and I remember thinking no bugger's going to go to that. I wonder how it turned out?"

Muriel Elsworth; I served Dana in the shop once. Violet wasn't there at the time, she went mad, she said, 'trust me to be away when she came in.'

In the shop itself, chaos had taken over once again especially in the upstairs room where thousands of 78 rpm records were all over the place with Violet inviting customers to conduct their own search for a record.

In fact it was quite easy to understand how one customer that Violet recalled had spent three weeks at the shop searching for one particular old classical record. Arriving everyday at the shop with sandwiches and flask he eventually found the record he was after! Thankfully Violet recruited Phil Booth to help make things easier and handed the unenviable task of categorising all the discs to him.

Violet would also be seen annually when she entered a float in the annual Sheffield Lord Mayor's parade. This would see a convoy of lorries all dressed up with designs pertaining to the many Sheffield businesses. On Violet's float various eras of pop music were depicted by members of her staff in fancy dress. **Muriel Elsworth;** "I was in all the Charleston gear". Rockin' piano man **Chuck Fowler** was also on it alongside **Gaspin' Gus**, complete with his disco decks. Violet herself was also aboard the float, sitting in a rocking chair at the back of the truck looking rather majestic as though she was the Lady Mayoress herself! Another year Gus was stood on a lorry with disco decks - shouting to the crowds to throw their money up for the various charities as he played records loudly.

Violet's float gets ready outside her shop for the Lord Mayor's Parade

Gus with Hank Taylor and his spouse Anne outside Vi's shop off The Moor

Cool Jazz at Violet May's

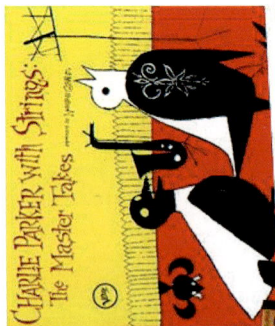

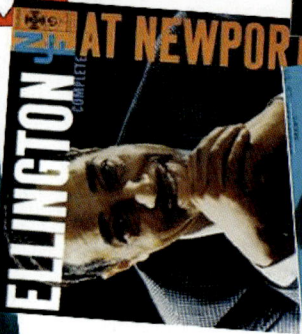

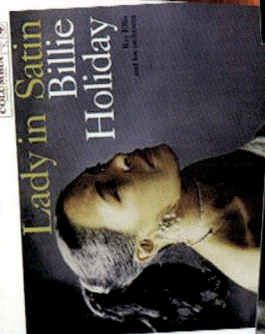

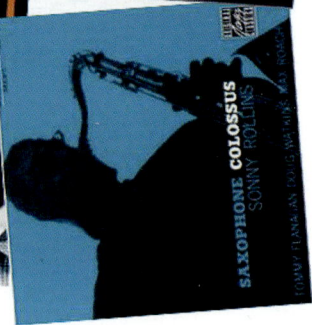

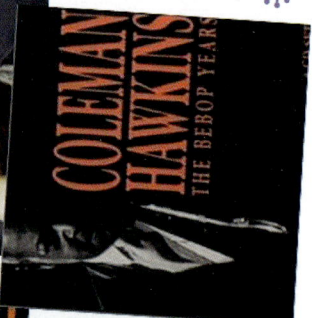

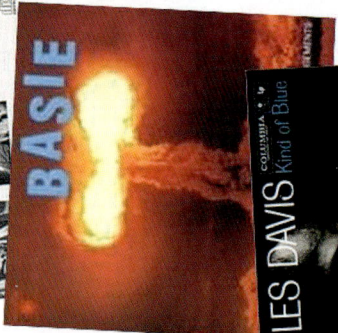

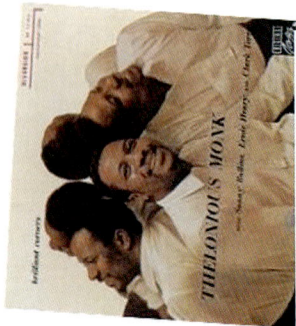

It's Trad Dad at Violet May's

Buried Treasure * & More Rare Gems

For many people, Violet May's shops were a virtual Aladdin's cave. **Mike Cocker;** "I thought the shop was a major find in that it had the stuff I liked, the stuff that had disappeared from the charts and was no longer played on Radio Luxembourg. The BBC as I'm sure you know had virtually no real pop discs. Since before the Beatles I'd always had a liking for American Rock'n'Roll - especially stuff like Dion, Del Shannon, Buddy Holly, Little Richard - and here was a place where you could get your hands on that kind of stuff. Sadly I didn't have much money - otherwise I'm sure I would have bought more. I can remember coming across Stagger Lee by Lloyd Price but couldn't spare the cash. Still regret it. Another prized purchase was a couple of Little Richard EP's. Also a battered copy of a Chess album 'Folk Festival of the Blues'. Still cherished but not played for so long. Must dig it out and find a turntable. "

Once paid a solo visit after school. Shop was virtually empty. I was looking for more 78's of American Ron's. She didn't have any to hand but she told me she had a room full of 78's on shelves upstairs. I ended up looking through 100's of old 78's looking for something by Elvis or Buddy etc. I did find a cracked copy of Rocking' Through The Rye by Bill Haley & His Comets but that was it. In retrospect I think she knew there was nothing up there but she was happy to let an eager fool like me have a second look just in case she missed something."

Glyn Senior; "I've always regarded Violet May's as my first great discovery; I've always been one for exploring and I just happened across it. That first impression was one of organised chaos. On the ground floor there were 45's everywhere with no attempt at classification, a lot of ex-jukebox records without the original centres, some new LP's but not chart stuff, mostly blues, jazz and folk."

Jenny Colley; "She had the kind of folk stuff that the other shops just didn't have."

Glyn Senior; "I found untold treasures at Violet's, not for financial gain but the musical knowledge which is exactly what I got and more. I can't remember everything I bought but among the standouts were two singles on the Columbia label by the classic 1964/5 Alexis Korner's Blues Incorporated line-up featuring Dick Heckstall-Smith, Danny Thompson and Herbie Goins. I think the A-sides were "I Need Your Loving" and "Little Baby". Those two absolutely brilliant singles on Pye International "Chicago Calling" by Cyril Davies' Allstars, "You'll Be Mine" by Long John Baldry, the B-side being "Up Above My Head (I Hear Music In The Air)" featuring an uncredited Rod Stewart. All those were second hand and cost about 3/6 (17½p) each. I bought a few American records mostly on the Sue and Chess labels. "Mockingbird" by Charlie & Inez Foxx, "Crossroads" by Homesick James, "Let It Rock" by Chuck Berry" and "Mona" by Bo Diddley" all come to mind but I think they were all new. Another great buy for me was an extremely battered copy of 'Blonde On Blonde' that I got for 12/6 (Sixty Two and half pence) and of course being a good Sheffield lad I showed some local support and got "I'll Cry Instead", by local gas fitter Joe Cocker." **Albert Clayton** "I got a lot of stuff there, all the "50 Guitars Of Tommy Garrett", I got them all from Violet's." **Dave 'Doc' Halliday**; "Frankie Miller - "Baby Rocked Her Dolly" on Starlite, I got that one there." **Mike Kersey:** "LP's I remember buying were; Elvis - Loving You 10" for 10 Shillings and also The Best Of Elvis on HMV 10" already a rarity even then and Violet knew that and charged accordingly. Also purchased Carl Perkins Dance Album on London (Autographed on the back where the original owner had written received at the Esquire Club, Sheffield') and the Carl Mann - Like Mann LP on London." **Phil Robinson**; "There were old 78's in the window with pictures printed on them - picture discs were NOT invented in the 70's!" **Dave Hawley**; "My mate Peter told me he'd seen the three Howlin' Wolf EP's in Violet's shop so I gave him the money and said 'go and buy all three'!" In 2006, **Dave Hawley** listed some his finds as follows; "These are just a few of the gems I managed to collect from Violet's over the years."

Dave Hawley

Arthur 'Big Boy' Crudup - *My Baby Left Me, 10" Album;*
Bone Walker - *Stormy Monday Blues, 10" Album;* **Fats Domino** - *A lot Of Dominoes (Rare album)*
Jack Hammer - *Switchblade Operator (Hammer wrote Great Balls Of Fire);* **Hank Penny** - *Country Album (His fiddle player was Boudleaux Bryant, co-writer with his wife Felice, of a number of Everly Brothers hits);* Three **Howlin' Wolf** EP's - *Smokestack Lightnin' (London American, - very rare)*

BO DIDDLEY

JOSH WHITE

B.B. KING LIVE IN COOK COUNTY JAIL

STEREO STEREO MUDDY WATERS AT NEWPORT 1960

SONNY BOY WILLIAMSON

LITTLE WALTER

SONNY TERRY & BROWNIE McGHEE

OTIS SPANN

T-BONE WALKER

BROKEN SOUL BLUES MEMPHIS SLIM

SISTER ROSETTA THARPE

Chuck Berry

WILLIE DIXON

HOWLIN' WOLF

BO DIDDLEY/CHUCK BERRY TWO GREAT GUITARS BO DIDDLEY/CHUCK BERRY

Get The Blues at Violet May's

Rare sheet music from Violet May's

Sheet music courtesy of Windmill Records

David Timmins; "I used to go to Violet Mays shop on City Road to buy records in the mid 1950's. My main interest in life at that time was jazz and Violet May was a very keen jazz fan who knew quite a few musicians. You could talk to her about the records and the backgrounds and techniques of the different jazz musicians. Her knowledge of jazz, and of course the records, was second to none. At that time there was very few imported records except the ones imported by Doug Dobel in London and the real fans in Sheffield got their fair share of these and it was Violet who got hold of them. When the American musicians started to come to Sheffield she attended every concert, always dressed for the occasion in a long dress and smoking her cigarettes through a long cigarette holder - every concert she had a different holder which was fascinating. Although never a beauty she was elegant and held a certain fascination, a real one off. She had a strong Sheffield accent with a gruffish voice, I suspect mainly caused by her strong smoking habit. Later she moved down to a shop on Broad Street opposite the Old Corn Exchange and then eventually moved to Matilda Street off the Moor.

She did adapt in her knowledge of music embracing all the different fashionable trends but her true love was Jazz. Violet attended all the jazz concerts at the City Hall and her knowledge of jazz music was extensive. I remember her guiding my choice of records knowing what little money I could afford and I thank her for developing my education in the music. I once picked up two metal master cut recordings of Charlie Parker from her shop on City Road, only to sell them back the following Saturday. At that young age I was disillusioned with them as they contained lots of false starts and stops. Little did I know that this was normal for 'The Bird', any jazz fan today would give his hind teeth for those two unique recordings today."

Hillbilly20; "I was a young 13 year old lad when I worked just behind the Moor for Violet in 1970. What an experience! It's fantastic to hear that others still remember this directly spoken but totally loveable person. I am so sorry to hear of her demise - but given her age and her chain smoking, it's hardly surprising. Does anyone know of the details of her death or where she is buried? I would like to pay my respects."

Shelby46; "Does anyone remember the "listening booths" in Violet Mays behind the Moor? I used to love going in there to listen before I bought records. It was a fabulous shop. As I recall, the door to the shop was on the corner, with the sales counter facing you as you turn slightly towards the right entering the shop. The booths were along that wall, going towards the back of the shop. You could give the staff a record to listen to, and they would play it for you. You had a set of headphones in the booth. That must have been very early 70's or late 60's."

Violet was seen very much as the head of the family and usually referred to as Grandma Barkworth. As she'd bequeathed most of her furniture to members of the family, to show this there would be the names of those who would receive them after she had gone stuck to the different items.

Fair Trade?* – Buying & Selling

As well as selling records, Violet would of course also buy them from customers, but could be hard-nosed if anybody took any items in to sell, resulting in some more memorable transactions.

Guitarist **Dave Hopper** recalls how Violet would operate; "I remember I took my best two Ricky Nelson albums into Violets to sell, hoping that I would get a good price for them. She looked at them and said, 'No, they aren't selling, now if you were to bring some Tom Jones in, I'd bite your hand off for them'. A bit later a bloke came in the shop and had some Tom Jones' albums to sell, which made me interested to see what Violet would say. She looked at them and said, 'Nah, these aren't selling; now if you had some Elvis, I'd bite your hand off'!!! **Dave Brennan** also recalls Violet's buying and selling tactics; "When I first went into her shop it was for 78's and I soon learned her ways of putting the price up if you looked interested. The cheapest way to buy a record was to study it for a bit, capturing her attention and then let her see you put the record back. She'd then say, 'You can 'ave it for one and six! One of the things I collected beside jazz and blues was early recordings of opera singers and one day she showed me glowingly a new range of Italian imports of 45's that had just come in. It was a small specialist Italian label and she emphasised that they were very rare (and consequently pricey). I bought one by Alessandro Bonci, a great tenor who had preceded Caruso. I had read that his recordings were very rare in this country and therefore expensive. When I heard Bonci I didn't like his quivery style at all and I took the record back the following week to part exchange it. This time there was no glowing look at the record but a shake of the head. 'I can't allow you owt on that, they're ten a penny them.' She'd obviously forgotten I'd bought it there the previous week."

Sheffield saxophonist **Bob Swift** recalls. "I remember this one bloke taking in his collection of Mario Lanza records. They were in pristine condition and he was obviously proud of them. But after examining them Violet just said 'what have you been doing, rolling them down the road?!' which of course indicated that she wasn't going to give the poor bloke much for them."

Mike Cocker; "I once sold her some 45's of Cliff Richard and other stuff too MOR e.g. Acker Bilk, acquired when I bought my second hand hfsx record player. I remember thinking that the price she was offering was a bit mean and far less than the price she was selling at; I hadn't grasped the basics of economic theory and practice at that point. But I think I did an exchange deal in which I got about 3 or 4 78's of Buddy Holly and Elvis Presley. Must get them out and play them.

Roger Harrison recalls Violet's wrath at losing a sale "I was stood behind this bloke who wanted to sell Violet a copy of Chuck Berry's album 'One Dozen Berries' which I wanted myself. Anyway she only offered about £3.00, then went into the back of the shop. I told the bloke I'd give him £4.00 for it as I really wanted the LP. When Violet came back the bloke told her he'd sold the album to me which made her go crazy and start shouting at me and she threw me out of the shop!"

Mike Evison; "I suppose I discovered Violet May's Shop somewhere near the bottom of Duke Street where the Park roundabout is now, when I was 15 in 1968. Initially I bought mainly singles and EP's, but as I got paid more as an apprentice electrician, I graduated to albums. By the time Violet had opened her Matilda Street shop, my visits became a weekly ritual. It was not unusual for me to buy 6 albums every Saturday. It got such a problem for my mother, that I had to sneak them into the house when she wasn't looking. One memorable visit was when I was in her shop and someone came in with a pile of albums, which wasn't unusual in those days. It was always a good idea to get them as soon as they arrived, before anyone else had their pick of them.

On this day, Violet was looking through them and came across the "Two Virgins" by John & Yoko Lennon. In those days I lived for John Lennon. When Violet saw the nudes on the cover, she flipped and said that she had to get it out of her shop before they closed her down. I asked her if I could buy it. She said give us a quid and take it away quickly. I still have that album. Musically it is rubbish but it is worth a lot more than a quid now."

It was usually in the week when Violet bought any records as **Mike Kersey** recalled. "In 1968 I went to Rimini, Italy, with a couple of friends with the idea of getting a job, but to no avail and returned after about 3 weeks absolutely broke and owing money, but while I was there I had bought lots of Italian Singles and EP's with fabulous picture sleeves and, desperate for money decided I would sell some of these to Violet and made the mistake of taking them to her on a Saturday Morning to be greeted with 'I'm not buying any records today - far too busy.' I was so embarrassed with all the people in the shop looking on and began walking back to the door when she shouted 'Bring them back I might as well look at them while you're here.' She looked through and then pushed a few notes in my hand. When I was out of the shop and counted the money it was nothing compared to what they were worth and I decided then I would not be selling any more records to her. I later learned that she did this on a regular basis to buy at good prices.

In the 70's I was starting to sell records myself on a Sunday Market and by Mail Order with ads in Record Mart and later Buygone Magazine and was buying still quite a lot from Violet but more to resell rather than for my own collection. I was still picking up quite a few bargains including some Joe Meek Rarities and quite a few good EP's.

Quite a lot of bargains were to be found in the Jazz EP section as some good R&B EP's used to end up in there, always used to be a lot of the Chuck Berry & Bo Diddley EP's too at good prices. At this time she started looking carefully at what I was buying and shortly after Chuck and Bo disappeared from the Jazz Section and made their way to the rarities box along with most of the other R&B EP's. She would look through what I was buying and tilt her glasses over her nose and look up at me and say - you know what you're buying don't you."

Stuart Mason; "Me and my three mates used to go to a shop in Chesterfield run by this old straight-faced guy who looked like Buster Keaton and buy up some of the records he was selling cheap and took them back to Violet's to sell. On one occasion the four of us all bought the same record and took them to Violets. When she saw they were all the same she went crazy, even though we tried to tell her they were all different versions!"

Hank Taylor still owes her a fiver!!! "The last time I visited the shop on Matilda Street was around 1970 or '71 when I purchased some albums by Fats Domino and Django Reinhardt, but came up £5 short. Vi agreed to me sending it on later but I never did. I often think about that today, sorry Vi!" Knowing who and what Violet was I think she may yet get it!

PHILIPS

LONDON
AMERICAN RECORDINGS
45 R.P.M.
E/T
45-HL
8886
LITTLE SUZIE
ENS

VIOLET MAY
Matilda Street, Sheffield
(Record Collector's Corner)

And For All The Following Items

Records
Record Players
Tape Recorders
Electrical Goods
Toys
Stationary
Books
Clothes
Christmas
Decorations
Bikes
Gramophone
Needles

Musical
Instruments
Cassette Tapes
Programmes
Catalogues
Light Bulbs
Batteries
Plugs
Sheet Music
Reel-To-Reel
Tapes
Framed Pictures
Stylus

Plus Lots More!

SONGSTER
STEEL
PICK-UP NEEDLES
SHEFFIELD MANUFACTURE
CONTENTS 100

Two Shades of Violet - Temperament

Looking somewhat radiant amongst the bargains

It should be noted that whenever one visited Violet's shop you never knew what frame of mind she'd be in and upon entering the shop it would never guarantee you a friendly welcome as she eyed-up every customer who came in the place. **Dave Manvell** remembers, "Whenever I went in she always seemed bad-tempered. She always asked you what you were looking for and sometimes if you were only browsing she'd tell you to 'get out if you're not going to buy anything'!" **Mike Cocker;** "To me, Violet May looked like a grandmother type who definitely belonged to the previous era. I can remember her sorting records behind her counter in a crowded and noisy shop one Saturday and looking outraged at someone kissing his girlfriend. Without stopping what she was doing she called loudly across the shop words to the effect of 'None of that in here'. The kissing stopped." As her daughter **Joyce Macdonald** observed, "She was a Virgo and very nit-picky. She used to say 'do not correct adults'." **Brian Monk** recalls his Aunt Violet; "Very different, most people found her hard work, she was a very strong, independent lady. I always got on very well with her."

Violet's presence could be most inhibiting as **Phil Robinson** recalls; ""Walking into the shop was a bit like going into a church, as you didn't talk to anybody else or make a noise, otherwise she'd embarrass you by asking if you'd come into the shop just for a chat, or to buy something?" **Mike Kersey:** "I was always a bit nervous of her as a schoolkid and as a teenager, one of the first things she'd say to me if I was carrying a bag would be 'Give me that bag before you look round', I thought she was picking on me until I heard her say the same thing to others, she really was quite frightening at times." **Jenny Colley;** "Sometimes she was so aggressive, we'd nickname her 'Violent May'!" **Dave Berry;** "Maybe it was because she'd heard of me, but Violet was always very nice and polite with me."

Carrier bags were taboo and if you had one she would demand that you left it with her behind the counter, almost insinuating that you would be tempted to slide something into it, even though some may have done at one time or another!

Glyn Senior; "I seem to recall entering the shop with my mate and Violet turned to one of her staff and said she was expecting the CID in to take a statement from her regarding some shoplifters she had bagged. I thought to myself; 'Aye, aye, she's giving us a veiled threat not to pinch owt'." **Phil Robinson** recalls another warning sign, "I went in the shop one day and she had pinned up an album cover with a note attached saying 'whoever stole this album, here is the cover'."

As well as being very abrupt alternatively she could be nice as pie. However, knowing what she could be like, made you actually feel a bit uneasy. One way of telling if you were OK with her was when she would speak to you by just mouthing the words, exaggeratedly, and not making a noise, as though she didn't want anybody else to hear what she was saying! **Dave Hawley;** "She was always nice to me, except once when I said the wrong thing when I asked her where she got her records from, to which she snapped back at me, "I'll get em' and you buy them". **Mike Cocker;** "She always came to me if she had anything I would like. But if you hadn't got enough money, you could pay in instalments. She was a business woman". **Dave Theaker;** "Violet was always fine with me. She never knew my name but she always recognised me when I came in and knew what kind of music I liked." **Albert Clayton;** "I used to call in her shop on my way home from the match and walk in about twenty-to-six and she'd look at the clock and then give me a funny look and ask if I was after anything special to which I'd say some particular artist and she'd say abruptly, 'No!, I've none of theirs'. But after a few minutes she'd come round the front of the counter and say 'if you want to come round the back of the counter, there may be some records you'd be interested in'." However **Ron Blythe** remembers a more trustworthy Violet; "She used to let me take records out of the shop to sell at where I worked".

Dave Brennan "To me as a young and enthusiastic record collector the shop itself was an Aladdin's cave. However my toes still curl up when I think about my encounters with the little barbed tongued sentry called Violet who guarded it. When Rotherham Libraries first set up a record lending library I was asked to select the LP for the jazz section. They had a budget and I said it would go further if they bought the records second-hand from Violet May's, they'd get many deleted items too. One Saturday morning I took two of the library staff over to have a quick look round the shop (They were on overtime!). They proceeded to catalogue every one of the thousands of jazz LP in the shop, examining their condition and painstakingly logging the details. The whole shop was disrupted, not to mention the customers and Violet was spitting blood.

I kept trying to calm her by telling her she'd get a big order out of it! In the event they didn't buy anything. They said they weren't in good enough condition. I told Violet the next time I was in the shop and I think for Violet that was the last straw as far as I was concerned!" Indeed, Violet was something of a paradox when it came to business as daughter **Joyce Macdonald** explains; "Although she was a successful business woman, she was also utterly stupid when it came to business too. She was both brilliant at business and rubbish at business." **Phil Robinson;** "I don't think she knew much about music, but she had an unerring instinct, and seemed to know the value of everything!"

Violet could also be quite benevolent too as the mood took her as **Muriel Elsworth** recalled; "Prisoners were having a concert and they were dressing up as women and they wanted a record 'Sisters, Sisters' (by The Beverley Sisters) and they wrote to her and asked if she could get it. She got it and sent it and they said 'thank you very much, how much do we owe you?' And she said 'no, it's a pleasure and she gave it them." **Dave Theaker;** "I never sold any records to her but I was often there when people were trying to sell her stuff. She could be quite hard and always paid the lowest prices, but I do recall one thing she said. It was to a lady who was trying to sell her a radio and Violet said, 'I don't buy for two and sell for ten', and it's true, she never did. I always thought her prices were very reasonable." Violet would also buy much of her stock from a warehouse in Manchester, usually taken either by son Peter or regular taxi driver Barry. However, as **Mike Cocker** recalled, she preferred her customers to think otherwise "I remember her telling me she'd just been to New York (I think by boat) on a record buying trip (and probably holiday). No idea what she bought or where she went though." **Dave Theaker** also recalls another of Vi's sidelines; "She had a sideline taping records for people. She used to put a mike beside a record player and tape onto a reel-to-reel tape-recorder. I can't imagine what she charged but the quality must have been appalling." So there you have it, Sheffield's fore-runner to Napster.

Violet's evenings out usually involved the services of Chauffer Barry - her regular taxi driver. He would arrive at the shop and take her either to her home or off to a jazz concert, record warehouse or exhibition of some sort. She always dressed up for these occasions in a long evening gown and smart looking coat. On occasion Violet would also be escorted by her nephew **Brian Monk;** "If I was near Sheffield, which sadly was not often, I would take Violet out to a concert, she loved Big Band Jazz, I think the last we saw was Buddy Rich at Sheffield City Hall."

A load of patter from the king of flannel for Violet at the opening night of the Sun Sound Club at the Staniforth Arms Darnall

One evening out in April 1968 saw Violet make a public appearance at the Staniforth Arms, Darnall. Here she helped to launch the re-opening of The Sun Sound Club, after a nine month closure. For the occasion, Violet graciously supplied both champagne and a cine film that night and a 1 minute 30 second silent movie was filmed by **Alan 'Happy Snaps' McClean** and features performers Steve Denton, Dave Hawley, Dave 'Cannon' Smith, Alan Wood, DJ Gaspin' Gus and Violet herself smiling constantly and obviously enjoying the VIP status she was accorded for the night. **Gus;** "What a great pity that we didn't have the facility for sound in those days - I could have heard me'self slurring down the mike." However, the film has thankfully since been transferred to VHS tape and then to DVD in order to preserve this little piece of Sheffield history.

Sun Sound member **Mike Kersey** also remembers the occasion; "I remember seeing her at The Sun Sound Club on Staniforth Road looking very smart in a black leather skirt and speaking to her I found her to be soft spoken and really nice, completely different to how she was in the shop."

Leader of Rotherham's celebrated Jubilee Jazz Band **Dave Brennan** (opposite top right) also recalled another of Violet's public appearances. Dave presented Now You Has Jazz on Radio Sheffield, 1975-89 and recalls the time when Violet took to the airwaves - almost! "Violet was the guest on my weekly Jazz Programme on BBC Radio Sheffield and I can truthfully say she caused me my most uncomfortable moments in about 15 years of doing the programme. I was a regular in the shop from being a teenager over 50 years ago and I still have many of the 78's I bought then. She used to treat me with disdain until she started to notice that a lot of customers coming into the shop knew me and she found out I was a bandleader and later a broadcaster. After that she became quite chatty. She used to tell me stories about all the famous jazz and blues artists who had been in the shop when appearing at the City Hall.

One story was about the blues singer Jimmy Rushing who had been searching for many years for one of his early recordings that he had never heard and he found it in the shop. There was a similar story about Chris Barber who was a great record collector and was always searching for early jazz rarities, which of course he'd found nowhere else in the country but had found plenty in Violet May's. The stories went on and I decided we could make a great programme talking about it and I went to a lot of trouble with the help of the BBC Gramophone Library in London to search out the vital recordings to accompany the chat. It was a bank holiday and I had been told that the programme was scheduled to start at 6.30pm and I had booked Violet a taxi accordingly. I was driving to Radio Sheffield along the Parkway when I heard Tony Capstick announce, 'After the news it's Dave Brennan'. The next five minutes was a blur! I arrived at the Studios on Westbourne Road to hear my signature tune being played on the car radio. I ran to the door to find it locked! After what seemed a lifetime I grabbed a record and waffled my way through until Violet came in scowling. I felt relieved, but the relief was short-lived! The conversation went like this;

(DB) 'Violet have you ever had any famous jazz musicians in your shop'?

(VM), (with scorn) 'Such as who?'

(DB) 'Well, er, such as blues singers or band leaders'

(VM)'Such as who'?

(DB) 'Well, for instance, Jimmy Rushing'?

(VM (with more disgust)'Oh ah, ee's been in'

(DB) 'Tell us about it'

(VM) 'What do you want me to say?'

This went on and I changed tack to Chris Barber.

Dave Brennan on air

(VM) (again with disgust) 'Oh ah, ee's been in an'all.'

This went on and the clock seemed to go backwards.

(DB) 'Did he buy any special records?'

(VM) Oh ah, 'e bought a record'.

Eventually, about half way through the rest of the programme, she stood up and said, 'Am gooin' nah, a've got summat in't oven. Can you get me a taxi'?"

Indeed, one can only sympathise with Dave at the pressure Violet put him under!

Violet May — celebrated knowledge of music.

7/4/87

The place for sound advice

Stephen McClarence
Sheffielder

THE trendy gramophone granny of the pop world (that's what they called her) is in full agreement.

Sheffield's first lady of popular music (that's what they called her as well) is, indeed, categorical.

As Bradleys record shop announces its closure after 20 years in the city, she reckons the field is wide open for a bit of entrepreneurial enterprise.

"You'd have thought someone would have jumped on the bandwagon, wouldn't you?" she poses from her Sharrow home. "You'd have thought someone would have set up a collector's shop."

Well you would if you were Violet May.

Violet May — Mrs. Violet Barkworth in her life away from the record browsers — belongs to the golden age of Sheffield record collecting. More accurately, she *was* the golden age of Sheffield record collecting.

Her now-closed shop in Matilda Street, jampacked with 78s and wooden boxes of singles stencilled Dance Tempo, American Tamla, Warner Bros and Reprise . . . her shop before that in Duke Street,

its attic stacked with shellac . . . before that in South Street, before that in The Pavement . . . They were "Meccas of Music" (another quote from the archives), the lot of them.

Where are those meccas now? Where does the discerning record collector go?

Time was when Bradleys was full of imported specialist records. If you wanted a disc of ceremonial Afghan wedding music, they may just have had it in stock. If not, they would have known a little shop in Kabul that *probably* had a copy in the basement.

But now, sadly, most of the city's major record shops belong to national chains. Unless you want pop or the most tiresomely mainstream classical and jazz, there is practically nowhere very interesting in Sheffield.

Practically. True, a handful of shops have stocks more enterprising than Barry Manilow, Dave Brubeck, James Galway, The Human League and Kiri te Kanawa.

And if you order, they can get. But who wants to order? The dedicated collector wants the record in his hands. It's the thrill of the chase, the joy of

capture after years of pursuit.

Nor does the dedicated collector want to browse in a flashy glossy sub-amusement arcade, with heavy metal thumping out of the speaker on your left and Dave Brubeck (there is no escape from Take Five) clattering out of the speaker on your right.

None of Sheffield's record shops aspire to the proper hallowed atmosphere of a proper hallowed collector's shop. There are, of course, plenty of them in London — cluttered, dusty places on the whole, full of cardboard boxes and cabinets no one ever quite got round to painting.

Curious-looking men (very few curious-looking women) sift edgily through teetering piles of records, gingerly edge them out of their sleeves and peer aggressively, accusingly, at specks of dust.

The conversation is all matrix numbers, snide references to inferior pressings of Jelly Roll Morton or Tetrazzini, the unique charisma of early Perry Como, the Ellington acoustics they once picked up in a back room in Basingstoke, the fatuous foolishness of so-called dealers who think a battered stack of Caruso soup plates are worth a fortune. They rarely mention Compact Discs. They are not terribly sure what Compact Discs are.

On a good afternoon, it was like this at Violet Mays. Particularly when the lady herself, the shrewdest of business-women, was in charge. (Which she was upto 1978, though the shop carried on under her name until 1985.)

The collectors came from all over the country to sift through the 28,000 78s piled challengingly

high in the upstairs room, naturally, it goes without saying, in no particular order. One collector came to search every day for a week, clutching flask and sandwiches. After six days, he unearthed the disc he wanted, and, as a sort of tribute, Violet May gave it him.

She was (indeed, is) celebrated for her knowledge of popular music. She astonished her grand-children with her appreciation of Johnny Rotten. One afternoon, a gent from Fulham Football Club rang up and asked if she had a particular record. He wasn't sure what it was, but if he hummed a bit, would she be able to . . . She found the record, played it over the telephone, and sent it off by the next post.

"Even now I've retired, I get people ringing me up," says the Trendy Granny (now, at 76, a Trendy Great-Granny). "But all I've got is a few 78s of Bill Haley. I sold off most of my 78s stock to a London dealer.

"I miss it all dreadfully. I'm still capable of running a shop, you know."

Violet May, gramophone granny, come out of retirement. Sheffield has need of you.

The End of an Era

In 1978, at the age of 68 Violet decided to cease business, mainly due to her failing health, and on her Doctor's advice. "The shop has been my lifeblood", she told The Star's local historian **Peter Harvey**. "It got to the stage where money didn't matter so much. My customers are like friends and I have made a lot of friends in the last 22 years. The schoolchildren who used to come and buy records from me at Broad Street are grown up now and they still come to the shop. Sometimes they bring me chocolates and little presents." Indeed Violet was regarded with great affection by all those who had encountered her through the years.

Following in Vi's footsteps was Windmill Records' **Mike Kersey** "I opened my first shop in 1978 so I didn't go in Violet Mays very often but when I did she didn't seem to have anything very much in stock that was new, just what I'd seen before and customers who were coming in my shop were saying she didn't seem to be getting anything collectable anymore. At this time record collecting was starting to grow with regular Record Fairs in London, Nottingham, Manchester and Leeds and it was getting harder to find good records, you really had to go out and look for them and could not rely on people just bringing them in, so her decision to sell at this time was a very good one in my opinion."

However, Violet hadn't planned to completely stop as she commented in the Sheffield Star; "I couldn't stop altogether though. I shall still go to the shop part-time." Upon her retirement Violet and husband Bill moved in to a bungalow on Dalewood Road, Beauchief.

Singles, Albums, E.P.'s Telephone 21567

"Violet May"
Mr. K. JESSOP
RECORD COLLECTORS CORNER

An advert in a magazine called Format Guide for Dutch, Swiss and UK record shops and fairs from about 1983.

Grace Monk; "It broke her heart when she sold it to her shop assistant. The shop was her life - we often went there - and I loved her collectors' room upstairs." Violet sold the shop to Keith Jessop, son of her former assistant, Wilf. Unfortunately, under it's new ownership, the shop made an attempt to shake off some of its past and keep up with the times, clearly suffering from the new broom syndrome as **Muriel Elsworth** observed; "When he took over he couldn't cope with it, he wanted all the modern stuff." Indeed, it was obvious that such a hallowed place found it incongruous to now cater for customers with possibly less discerning tastes. The Matilda Street shop subsequently became a wool shop before becoming an emporium for sci-fi comics.

Two years later, another regular Star columnist Stephen McClarence noted the closure of another prominent Sheffield record shop, Bradley's, whilst his article, titled The Place For Sound Advice centred round Violet, and reminded everyone of her and her shops whilst also reiterating the important role she played with the comment 'Violet May, gramophone Granny, come out of retirement, Sheffield has need of you.'

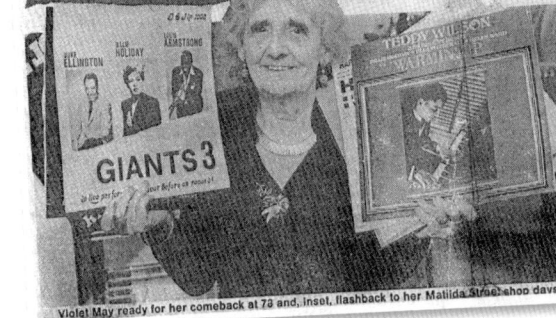

Violet blooming as she plans record comeback as an old 78

by SIMON IRWIN

SHEFFIELD'S most exciting re-release in years is about to be launched onto the city's record market . . . the return of Violet May's Record Collectors' Corner!

Violet May Barkworth, known as just Violet May to her many thousands of customers over the years, is making a return to selling 78s at the grand old age, ironically, of 78!

Hey-day

In her hey-day, Violet was known as the trendy gramophone granny or Sheffield's first lady of popular music, and she intends her return to be a glorious blast from the past.

She retired in 1978, but the Matilda Street shop did not close until 1985. At its peak, the old shop bulged with rare discs, including everything from classical music to Tamla and big-band classics.

Violet, continued: "I made my mind up a fortnight ago to go back into business. I expect to open on London Road in my new shop in about a month."

Grinning

Grinning as she lit yet another cigarette, she said: "I've had my letter confirming I've got the you."

Speaking at her Wincobank Avenue home, Wincobank, she said: "I'm too old to be starting out in business really, but I'm bored stiff sat here, doing nothing all day."

shop, if my references all right. They will be.

The core of her r stock — a few interesti looking boxes and pa ages, wrapped up brown paper — sits on floor of her front room

"There's a few hund good ones there, all c lectors' stuff," she said

Violet May has just c problem with her n venture: how to break news to her son.

'Surprise'

"He doesn't kn about it yet. It will co as a surprise," s laughed.

As she sits planning h comeback, Violet buz with life, excited to back into the hurly-bu of the retail world.

"It certainly beats s ting here, watching te vision. I'm really looki forward to seeing some my old customers," s revealed.

She has answered t call of The Star's Steph McClarence who said, a 1987 'Sheffielde column: "Violet Ma gramophone grann come out of retireme Sheffield has need you."

GIANTS 3

Violet May ready for her comeback at 78 and, inset, flashback to her Matilda Street shop days.

Working at Windmill Records shop in The Wicker, **Kenny Roper** recalls Violet coming in and enquiring about a job; "She just walked in off the street and had a look round, I was quite surprised to see her. I think she was just being a bit nosey. She said 'I could do with a little job'. I think she was getting bored." One can only surmise how it would be to have Violet working for somebody else. It's a good bet that she wouldn't want anybody telling her what to do.

Eventually, nine years after retiring, Violet May hit the headlines once again as she announced that she would be making a comeback to the record retail world! Still not in the best of health, Violet admitted "I'm too old to be starting out in business really, but I'm bored stiff sat here, doing nothing all day." She continued "I made my mind up a fortnight ago to go back into business. I expect to open on London Road in my new shop in about a month." Her new shop was to be down near the bottom of London Road, where her former manager, Phil Booth had set up a shop that specialised in 78 rpm records and vintage gramophones and record-players.

Grace Monk; "I remember when she was about 78 she rented a shop and tried to start again. My brother was away on holiday and didn't know so he was shocked on his return to find she had it all arranged, but of course she wasn't well enough to carry it through."

Mike Kersey; "A few years later when I used to advertise in local papers for records I had a phone call to go and look at some records and who should answer the door but Violet herself. She looked extremely frail and was struggling to walk even with the help of a walking stick. The first thing I thought was what a small house for someone who I thought would be quite wealthy and live somewhere quite posh. She was very nice and friendly and spoke about the times she had the shops and that it really was her life and wished she had never sold up, and that she was hoping to get back into the business again and open a shop. I didn't like saying anything to her but I knew that this would never happen, not only healthwise, but it was no longer possible to make a living just with a shop, certainly not in Sheffield anyway, Ken was working for me by this time and as well as the shop we were doing Markets, Record Fairs, Stalls at various Rock 'n' Roll Dances, and I was putting out Mail Order Sales catalogues every couple of months and believe me, I was only making a living wage, so I don't think she would have lasted long just with a shop. The records she wanted to sell me were only very average at best and I wouldn't normally have bought them but she told me what she wanted for them and I just gave her the money, I don't know whether it was because I just couldn't say no to her or I just felt sorry for her. I realised when I left how much respect I had for her, I now knew how hard it was - buying at the right price, finding good wholesalers, constantly on guard for shoplifters etc, etc. That was the last time I saw her."

The house on Cherry Tree Road, Nether Edge

Unfortunately it was just a few months later that another piece appeared in the Star stating that 80-year old Violet had had to abandon the idea of returning to work on doctor's orders as she was not in the best of health. "I haven't changed my mind about wanting to open up another shop - but the Doctor has changed it for me," said Violet. "I am disabled and the Doctor didn't think it was sensible for me to take two buses every day. I have decided to go along with what the Doctor has advised but I am very disappointed."

In 1984 Violet and Bill sold the house on Cherry Tree Road and moved to a bungalow at Dalewood Road, Meadow Head. From there they then went to a flat in Park Grange Avenue - although sadly they'd only been moved in a week when Bill died.

Peter Elsworth; "Then mother had burglars during a day out with us, so she wanted to get away after these events and moved back to Nether Edge to a flat on Sharrow Grange Crescent. This place was in need of a major revamp and she started ailing so decided to move to Wincobank Avenue to be near to us. 6 months before she died she tried to move again but I blocked it as I had done enough moving for her."

Bill Barkworth was remembered as a really meek and mild man as **Muriel Elsworth** recalls, "He was a lovely man. When he'd died and we was in the will Violet said, 'what do you want?' I said, it'd be nice to have a new three-piece suite if there's enough for it. So she said 'go and pick it' and we picked one of those red low cottage suites. We came back and she said 'I'll go with you tomorrow and pay for it'. However, on the return to the shop Violet became her usual dominant self. I said, 'we want that', showing her the one we'd picked. She said, 'you don't want that, you want that one over there' and she pointed to a horrible green great big one. The assistant said, you don't want to put up with that if they're buying it you, you want the one that what you want. Anyway, we had to have this three-piece suite." She also recalls more of Violet's domineering ways "She once gave us the deposit for a car, about £50.00. We used to take her to Manchester and she'd

Violet and Bill on a day out in the Peak District

say 'don't forget, I paid for this car', and she'd only give us the deposit!. She knew she could bully you. Walking into a light shop one day she demanded 'haven't you got a seat I can sit on, I can't stand like this' and she hadn't even said if she wanted to buy anything."

In her retirement Violet often thought of herself as some kind of a lady as daughter-in-law **Muriel Elsworth** recalled, "She would say 'I want to grow old like a Lady'." Also, with her delusions of grandeur, Violet wouldn't be averse to showing people up too as Muriel also remembers; "We were once in an ordinary café and the girl waitress was serving and served on the left instead of right and she (Violet) said, 'don't you know any different than that, you're supposed to serve from the other side'. And the poor lass said 'I've only just started today'. Anyway when she came round to me I said, 'I don't mind where I get it from love, as long as I get my dinner'. 'Don't speak like that' she (Violet) said, 'they've got to learn'."

Also in her retirement Violet turned her attention towards painting. "I've been doing them for years," she told the Sheffield Telegraph, "It's something inside me". **Muriel Elsworth;** "She could paint and gave us all paintings of our daughters, her own daughters, my daughter, everybody." However although she was a fine painter not all the pictures were hers and Violet wasn't averse to take somebody else's painting and put her name on it!

As Peter recalls "mother used to do some painting in her own right but never up to the standard needed for this painting, next thing we know she presented us with this painting saying she had done it for our anniversary, also saying where we should hang it. Every time she came to our house she'd make sure we had it up on view. She also used to do knitting, so she said, but I never saw her knit anything. Now and again she would fetch knitted jumpers etc, saying she had made them when you could tell they were shop bought - also apparently she gave a painting to Joyce and our daughter."

By the end of 1985 The Star reported that Violet's old shop on Matilda Street was due to close with the title 'Pop shop shuts up' - Violet's name had been retained for the business up to this time. "It was very sad to see the shop closing" Violet commented. "I enjoyed every minute I was in the music business and the shop will always have special memories for me." Somewhat ominously, owner Keith Jessop declined to offer any comment on the situation.

In 1993 the Sheffield Telegraph recognised her as she was nominated in a search for Britain's top retired person, although it's not reported if she won.

After moving to a flat on Wincobank Avenue - by this time Violet was not able to get about because of leg trouble and a blood disorder through smoking, and giving her son Peter due credit via Sheffield Star, Violet nominated him for a British Health Care Award in 1995 stating that she could not carry on without the help he gave her. "My son is quiet and unassuming. But he is always there when needed. He visits me and takes me for days out in his car."

GRAPH NEWS

Honour for Violet May

FOR years, Violet May's was a legendary record shop among collectors in Sheffield and much further afield.

Now, in retirement at her home in Wincobank, she is not forgotten. For Violet May Barkworth – to use her full name – has been nominated in a search for Britain's top retired person. She still loves music, especially jazz and the Big Band sounds of the 1930s, with personal favourites Louis Armstrong and Benny Goodman.

And since retiring in 1978, her other great interest is painting in water colours. "I've been doing them for some years. It's something inside me," she says. Her subjects range from her husband, Bill, to flowers and animals.

But Violet, aged 83, of Wincobank Avenue, admits: "I miss the shop and the people." She was in her mid-40s when she turned her second-hand shop into a record collectors' paradise after somebody offered her a box of old 78s.

Not only did she build up a vast range of musical styles in the Matilda Street shop, but her knowledge became encyclopaedic, leading to the label of "Sheffield's Gramophone Granny".

"People I meet remember Violet May and the shop," she says. "I suppose it has become a bit of a legend."

Now she has another record in mind. She joins more than 150 entries in retirement awards backed by McCarthy & Stones, builders of retirement flats. The regional winner will be announced in the New Year and will receive £500.

Gramophone Granny: Violet May Barkworth

One year Peter and Muriel took Violet on holiday abroad and she was by now in a wheelchair. "We had this coloured lad looking after us and we were playing darts. 'I want to go' she says. Well the lad said, 'you're not able to get out of the wheelchair' and she just jumped up out of it and the lad said 'it's a miracle, Jesus, it's a miracle!'." Daughter Grace also recalls another special day out for Violet's 80th birthday, "Muriel organised an outing to Blackpool for the ladies at their club and asked us to go." Joyce. "We had a lovely day out and walking along the prom a jazz band was playing. We had Mam in a wheelchair we'd borrowed, she sat there eyes shining and singing along with them. One of the young men pulled her out of the chair and danced round holding her so her feet were off the ground, that made her day. I'll never forget her excitement at that."

'Gramophone granny' dies

By PETER KAY

ONE of the legends of Sheffield's music scene has died at the age of 84.

Violet May Barkworth (pictured) was no musician, but her name was known over a wide area thanks to the specialist second-hand record shops she ran for nearly 30 years.

She used to receive telephone calls from America asking if she could find a certain disc. At this end, up-and-coming performers such as Dave Berry would scour her racks for obscure American imports.

On one occasion, she was contacted by prisoners wanting to perform Sisters at a prison concert, but they couldn't find a copy of the Beverley Sisters' record to mime to. They knew who to turn to.

Everybody with an interest in music in the fifties, sixties and seventies knew Violet May who, in later years, was inevitably dubbed "Sheffield's Gramophone Granny".

She died last Saturday in the Northern General. Even in her last days in hospital she was recognised as a celebrity, her daughter-in-law, Muriel Elsworth said this week. "Everywhere she went, somebody would say 'I know her'."

Violet May was in her mid-forties when she turned a second-hand clothes shop into a record-collectors' paradise after somebody offered her a box of old 78s. In shops in South Road, Broad Lane and Matilda Street, she carried a vast range of musical styles and her knowledge of popular music was encyclopaedic.

Her personal favourite was jazz and the Big Band sounds of the Thirties, once meeting one of her heroes, Louis Armstrong, backstage at the City Hall.

After retirement to her Wincobank Avenue home in 1978, she developed another interest, water colour painting. She kept active to an extent that she was nominated two years ago for regional retirement awards.

But at the time she she admitted: "I miss the shop and the people". When she was in her 80s, collectors would still bring records for her to value.

She leaves two daughters and a son. A service will be held at St Thomas's Church, Wincobank, on Monday at 2.30pm followed by interment at Shiregreen Cemetery.

Farewell Violet May

On 4th August, 1995, Violet died at Northern General Hospital. Her death certificate said 'due to smoking', **Peter Elsworth**; "I'd never seen that before, it said 'a life-time smoker'." A heavy smoker most of her life, customers in her shop fondly remember her constantly smoking, using a variety of different cigarette holders whilst creating a smokey haze inside the shop! Despite their various misgivings, I suspect that all of Violet's family still look up to her with some admiration for her contribution to music as well as a mother.

Violet May's final place of rest is at Shiregreen Cemetery

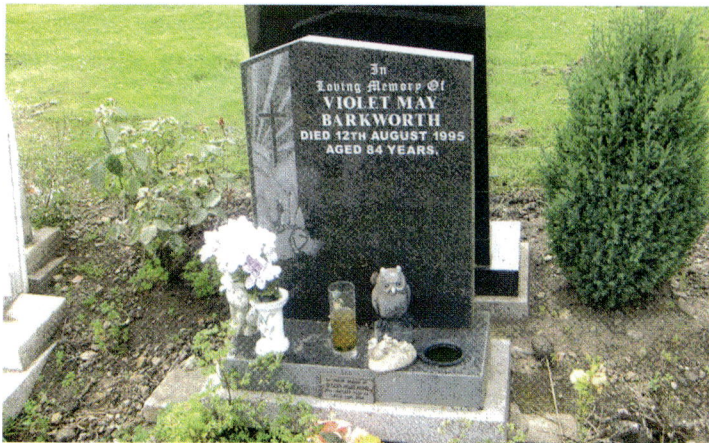

Violet's musical legacy has also been passed on to **Brian Monk,** Grace's son. "My son Brian has followed in her footsteps loving music." Indeed Violet encouraged Brian as a 15 year-old when he first took up the bass guitar, and bought him an amplifier for his birthday.

Brian Monk; "We were very close as I loved painting and was in the music industry. She gave me my first guitar, a Vox guitar and a small amp. I think it was for my 13th Birthday, she encouraged me to become a musician. And encouraged me to play, she sent me hundreds of unusual and mainstream albums, and never ever sent the same one twice." Brian recalls how he and Violet also shared a love for painting; "From an early age I loved painting and drawing, and Vi was always interested to see what I was doing. Been many years now since I painted, but she left me her brushes etc when she died, which I still have. One day I will start again."

Nowadays Brian Monk lives in Weston-Super-Mare where he runs his own recording studio which he built himself. "I played in various bands touring etc., between 1969 and 1980, then went into production and recording, working with artists like Eurythmics, Tears For Fears, Genesis and many others." Brian's studio is Horizontal Music Recording Studios in Somerset, to which his proud mother Grace adds; "It's fantastic."

Violet's other grandson, James McDonald has also had some success in the literary world with the publication of his book *Wordly Wise*, which looks at the origins of English words and phrases.

Violet (second from right) with husband Bill, daughters Grace and Joyce and son Peter

Violet and sister Ivy

Final Tributes

And so it remains, even though it is now forty years since Violet ran her shop there the lady will be remembered by many Sheffielders through her endeavours. Thanks to her, our musical knowledge and record collections are a lot better for the many visits to her various shops.

This is certainly true as verified by **Dave Theaker;** "In July '71 I packed up my job and moved to Kawasaki. I've been back to Sheffield loads of times and the last time I saw Violet would have been in May '74. I was on my way back to Japan and dropped in to buy a load of Biblical film soundtrack for a pal in Malaysia. She was a little surprised at my choice of music and we had a chat."
Mike Cocker; "With 20/20 hindsight I can now see it was a unique and special place run by a unique and special woman. Like so many things that have passed by, I should have paid more attention."

Over the years Violet's has enjoyed a wider reputation as **Muriel Elsworth** testifies, "No matter where you go, anywhere in the world, someone will say, 'I used to go there'." **Grace Monk;** "I had a guest house for 48 years and if any guests came from Sheffield I always asked them if they knew Violet May's shop - and they always did!"

Following in Violet's footsteps was collector's shop owner **Mike Kersey;** "I can't remember whether I actually thought at the time that at some time I would like to have shops like hers selling records, but it's likely it was on my mind as I used to love cleaning the records and sleeves and displaying all the records that I had bought - I loved vinyl then and still love vinyl now."

Looking back on Violet's role in Sheffield life, the last words come appropriately from the lady herself, in this post script taken from a letter to her daughter Grace in 1985;

"Enclosed is a paper cutting of your Mam, they didn't forget me after 7 years. Lovely of them (end of an era) I feel proud after all the years of hard work, I feel respected and it means a lot; work more than money."

Violet's Name Revived

Possibly seen as a tribute but here in 2009, a new Sheffield band has emerged calling themselves **The Violet May**.

Apparently, some of the band's elders were Violet May customers and whilst their musical output is of the modern variety, it's a good bet that Violet herself would have at least given it a listen, especially if she thought there may be some money to made from it!

Therefore, it's good to see her name living on as part of the Sheffield music scene in the 21st century.

THE VIOLET MAY

POSTER DESIGN BY M. F. BEDFORD ©2008 • www.myspace.com/frogandparrot

The Violet May, above
The Forum on Wednesday

TO look at him these days you might not recognise Chris McClure as the face from the cover of the Arctic Monkeys debut album.

A few years on from that record-breaking record and the brother of The Reverend Jon McClure is fronting his own rather promising band, featuring a few familiar talents from the Sheffield music parade and here playing a stones throw from the scene of their inaugural gig at the Frog & Parrot.

Alongside the Fugitives, The Violet May are giving a live set tomorrow as part of a "brand re-launch" for city-based rock photographer Tracey Welch, who took this shot of them.

As well as the music you can peruse an exhibition of her music assignments and corporate work in a joint display with up and coming Sheffield-based graphic designer Daniel Rose who has designed Tracey's fresh look. Exhibition runs until July 5.

David Dunn

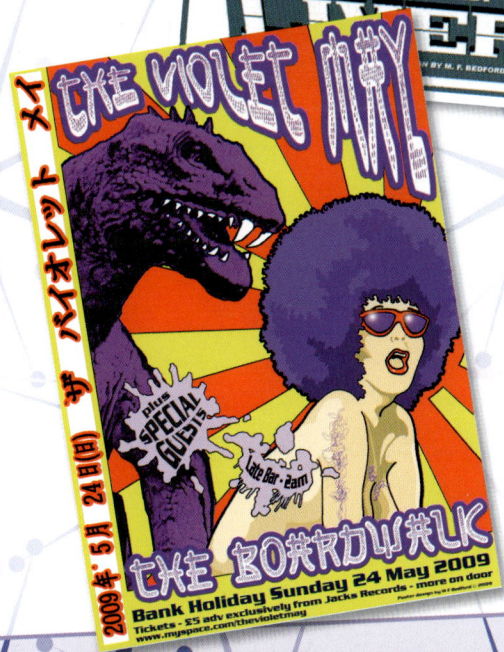

Poster art courtesy of Martin Bedford

Notes on Contributors

J.P. Bean

One time folk/country singer and guitarist and noted author with several books to his credit including the acclaimed Sheffield Gang Wars.

Dave Berry

Iconic 60's performer and Sheffield's first international star.

Ron Blythe

Sheffield musician who worked with artists like Dave Hawley, Glen Dale and is an established solo act.

Dave Brennan

Banjoist and leader of his own jazz band and one time radio presenter with his own jazz programme on BBC Radio Sheffield.

Phil Brodie

Former guitarist with Bitter Suite and fronting his own blues/rock band.

Pete Carson

Amateur photographer and record collector, now sadly passed away.

Albert Clayton

Collector and former secretary of the Slim Whitman Appreciation Society.

Joe Cocker

World renowned white soul singer now living in Colorado, USA.

Mike Cocker

Former Sheffielder and Television producer whose credits include 'The Bill'.

Jenny Colley

Sheffield singer and musician.

Peter Elsworth

Violet's son, now living in Wincobank, Sheffield.

Muriel Elsworth

Violet's daughter-in-law married to Peter.

Mike Evison

Sheffield music fan and collector.

Dave 'Doc' Halliday

Rotherham music collector.

Roger Harrison

Veteran Sheffield drummer with several bands including Cherokees, The Daizies and Frank White. Roger sadly passed away June 2009.

Dave Hawley

Sheffield singer/guitarist who fronted his own band in the 60's and worked in a duo with Ron Blythe in the 70's. Sadly passed away in February 2007.

Howard Holmes

Sheffield music fan and collector.

Dave Hopper

Sheffield guitarist whose credentials include Joe Cocker, Chuck Fowler and Steve Denton.

Mike Kersey

Former proprietor of Windmill Records (The Wicker & Rockingham Street) still dealing in collector records via mail order.

Dave Manvell

Collector and author of a number of books on Sheffield including The Mojo Club.

Stuart Mason

Long time Sheffield collector.

Joyce MacDonald

Violet's daughter, now living in Goxhill, Humberside.

Brian Monk

Violet's nephew. Moved to London at the age of 15 and toured around the world as a musician. Now runs his own recording studio in Cornwall.

Grace Monk

Violet's daughter, now living in Weston-Super-Mare.

Phil Robinson

Ex-Sheffielder now living in Bath.

Kenny Roper

Former owner of Kenny's Records (The Wicker) and now retired.

Glyn Senior

Another ex-Sheffielder, now living and working in Japan.

Chris Spedding

Former guitarist with Sheffield band The Vulcans who moved to London in 1961 and became a well-respected session musician as well as enjoying his own chart success with *"Motorbikin'."*

Alan Spinks

Former resident of Park Hill and school pal of John Firminger.

Bob Swift

Sheffield musician playing saxophone with several combos.

John 'Hank' Taylor

Former London East-ender, now living in Westcliffe-on-Sea and still collecting the music.

Dave Theaker

Former resident of Park Hill now teaching English in Japan.

David Timmins

Another Sheffield collector and Violet May patron.

Alan Wood

Sheffield musician and established agent and manager.

Photograph courtesy of Jack Wrigley

ADDENDUM

It was Wilf Jessop, who played a pivotal role in the Violet May story when he originally brought a box of 78 records to sell in her Duke Street shop in the mid 50's and in doing so, started her career off selling records.

Wilf and his family were very close friends of Violet and her family and, albeit unpaid, he also helped out in a number of her shops. These would benefit by his considerable knowledge of music, especially in the jazz and classical fields, contributing towards her shop's success.

When Violet eventually sold up and retired in 1978, it was Wilf's son, Keith who bought the Matilda Street shop. In 1968 he had become a DJ , and was well known around the city's nightclubs alongside many famous Radio personalities. With his own disco show, Keith was also an early driving force behind the Northern Soul movement in and around the local area.

Taking over Violet's shop, Keith and his Dad, Wilf, had a mammoth task on their hands in view of the often chaotic condition of the shop under Violet's supervision, (as recalled by many). However, after maximum effort, they regained some semblance of order amongst the thousands of dusty old records in stock and soon had the shop back in full-flow.

Contrary to what it said in the Violet May book about Keith not being able to cope with the business and trying to brush away some of the past with a more up-to-date approach, he did in fact continue much in the tradition of Violet whilst also integrating with current trends. His main problem however, was when The Moor became pedestrianised and for many, less accessible, which caused a steady decline in customers.

Since 1999 Keith and his wife Mary have lived out on the Welsh Coast, but maintain their ties with Sheffield.

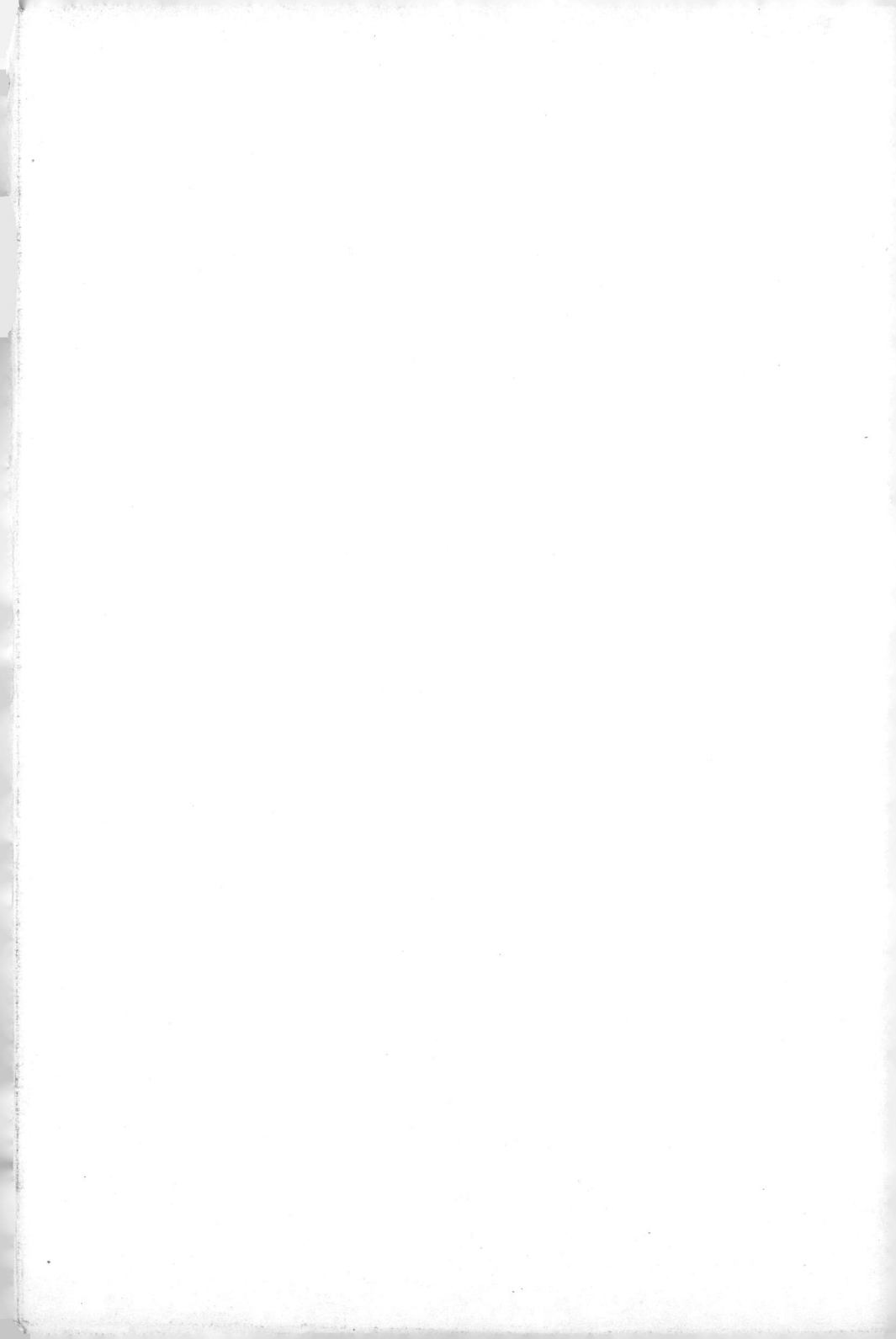